Unusual
Topics

Unusual Topics

A Practical Study of Some
of the Most Unusual
Subjects in the Bible

Robert E. McNeill

EDITOR, GEORGE M. BOWMAN

WINEPRESS **WP** PUBLISHING

Cover Design by Ragont Design.

Packaged by WinePress Publishing, PO Box 428, Enumclaw, WA 98022. The views expressed or implied in this work do not necessarily reflect those of WinePress Publishing. The author is ultimately responsible for the design, content, and editorial accuracy of this work.

ISBN 13: 978-157921-498-2
ISBN 10: 1-57921-498-3
Library of Congress Catalog Card Number: 2002112130

Printed in China.
APC-FT5219

A Quiver Full

This book is dedicated to my six children: **Bob**, **David**, **Barbara**, **Bonita**, **Douglas**, and **Daniel**, all of whom are believers in Jesus Christ and are married to believers; are college graduates, and married to college graduates. I had the honor and privilege of baptizing and marrying each one of them. They have so far given my wife, Jeanne, and me two exceptional grandsons and nine beautiful granddaughters.

> Lo, children are an heritage of the LORD: and the fruit of the womb is his reward. As arrows are in the hand of a mighty man; so are children of the youth. Happy is the man that hath his quiver full of them. (Psalm 127:3–5)

Thank you, Holy Spirit, for inspiring such words of God-given rights, special promises, and for a half-century of wonderful happiness.

The Gospel and Nothing Else

I have my own opinion that there is no such thing as preaching Christ and him crucified, unless we preach what is now called Calvinism. It is a nickname to call it Calvinism. Calvinism is the Gospel and nothing else. I do not believe we can preach the Gospel . . . unless we preach the sovereignty of God in his dispensation of grace, nor unless we exalt the electing, unchangeable, eternal, immutable, conquering love of Jehovah.

Nor do I think we can preach the Gospel unless we base it upon the special and particular redemption of his elect and chosen people which Christ wrought out upon the cross, nor can I comprehend a Gospel which lets saints fall away after they are called.

—Charles Haddon Spurgeon (emphasis added)

Zeal for maintaining the doctrines of the Gospel . . . will make a man hate unscriptural teaching, just as he hates sin. It will make him regard religious error as a pestilence which must be checked, whatever may be the cost.

—Bishop John Ryle

Table of Contents

Introduction

WE GET ALONG FAMOUSLY!

Most of us have questions about various topics in the Bible, but rarely invest the time and effort to find the answers. Dr. McNeill is one of those rare Bible scholars who has done the necessary digging to provide his readers with information about some *Unusual Topics*.

His book is loaded with exciting ideas and anecdotes that make it a genuine page-turner. As his editor and book organizer, I found that I wanted to get back to work on his manuscript and ideas as soon as possible each day.

I had such a good time working with Dr. McNeill on his book *God Indeed!* that when he suggested we work double harness again on this new volume, I jumped at the opportunity.

At the time he telephoned from Florida, saying he wanted me to edit a new book he was writing, I gladly put aside what I was doing in order to have the privilege and the pleasure of working with him again. Dr. McNeill provided the material to be included and asked me to edit what he had written and to design the layout of the book.

Some wonder how two men, living hundreds of miles apart, in two different countries, who have never met in person, can work together to produce a book. Well, it is not really so difficult when we both love the same Lord and Saviour, the same Bible, and the same doctrines of sovereign grace. In addition, we each have a sincere, mutual interest in advancing the sound doctrine that holds biblical truth in balance.

If you are anything like me and are eager for more information about the Word of God, you will find Dr. McNeill's ideas so profitable and interesting that, instead of turning on the television, you may want to curl up by the fireside and read this book!

Unusual Topics is a spiritual book. It is sound in doctrine, but more than that, it has been designed to edify and encourage you to take what you learn here and put it into practical use in your own Christian life. I pray that you will do so—even today!

—George M. Bowman, editor

CHAPTER ONE

Circumcision

Some years ago it was permitted to have Bible study in the public schools on a time-release basis. Once when a pastor was reading the Bible to a class of junior high and senior high boys and girls, the word "circumcision" was included in the passage he read.

Suddenly a girl student spoke up and asked, "What does circumcision mean?"

The pastor was taken aback by the question and especially by the fact that a high school girl did not know the meaning of the word. Somewhat embarrassed, he said, "Go home and sit down with your parents and have them explain the word to you."

That was good advice, and many parents would agree that he answered wisely. There was a possibility, however, from the pastor's answer, that others in that classroom would have gotten the idea that there was something "hush, hush" about circumcision—that it was a subject not to be discussed in public.

Knowledge of Circumcision Needed

This subject is so important, however, that without a knowledge of the meaning and background of circumcision one cannot rightly understand many important doctrines of the Bible. It seems to me that one could use medical terms and explain to a class of high school students exactly what the word means.

For example, the *Evangelical Dictionary of Theology* says that circumcision is "an operation performed on the male organ of propagation for the removal of the foreskin."[1] Both the Hebrew and Greek words translated "circumcision" in the Bible mean "to cut around—to remove the foreskin of the male penis by cutting around or encircling."

Remarkably, the Bible contains eighty-five references to circumcision. Four of the greatest men who ever lived were circumcised when they were eight days old. They were: the Lord Jesus Christ, Paul the Apostle, John the Baptist, and Isaac, the son of Abraham. Abraham was circumcised at the age of ninety-nine! Abraham's other son, Ishmael, was circumcised at age thirteen.

Timothy, an associate of Paul the Apostle, was circumcised by Paul when he was a young man. Although his mother was Jewish, he had not been circumcised as an infant because his father was a Greek. Knowing that Timothy *not* being circumcised would be offensive to most Jews, Paul circumcised him so as to remove what could have been a hindrance to the preaching of the Gospel among them.

To give us a better understanding of this *unusual topic* of the Bible, we'll look at the procedure's history, purpose, importance, confusion, and symbolism.

The History of Circumcision

The first reference to circumcision in the Bible is found in Genesis 17:10–14. Here is the Lord speaking to Abraham in that Genesis passage:

> This is my covenant, which ye shall keep, between me and you and thy seed after thee; Every man child among you shall be cir-

---

1. M. H. Woodstra, "Circumcision" in *Evangelical Dictionary of Theology* (Grand Rapids: Baker Book House, 1984), 245.

cumcised. And ye shall circumcise the flesh of your foreskin; and it shall be a token of the covenant betwixt me and you. And he that is eight days old shall be circumcised among you, every man child in your generations, he that is born in the house, or bought with money of any stranger, which is not of thy seed. He that is born in thy house, and he that is bought with thy money, must needs be circumcised: and my covenant shall be in your flesh for an ever-lasting covenant. And the uncircumcised man child whose flesh of his foreskin is not circumcised, that soul shall be cut off from his people; he hath broken my covenant. (Genesis 17:10–14)

According to *The New Bible Dictionary*, this passage is "the sole biblical account of the origin of Israelite circumcision. It was integrated into the Mosaic system in connection with the Passover (Exodus 12:44), and apparently continued throughout the Old Testament."[2]

Religious and Symbolic

Circumcision has been practiced in both civilized and savage cultures. These include Arabs, some African tribes, Christian Abyssinians, Australian blacks, Malaysians, some North American Indians, Aztecs, Mayas, Caribs, South American Indians, Jews, Moslems, and those living in Fiji, one of the Samoan Islands.

The original object of circumcision among the Hebrews was religious and symbolic. The Hebrews are different than any other race or group in that they always circumcise the male child on the eighth day after birth, even if it falls on their Sabbath. Other eastern nations have chosen other days. For example, the Arabs have chosen the seventh, fourteenth, twenty-first, and twenty-eighth day after birth.

Flavious Josephus, a Jewish historian of the first century A.D., however, said that in his day Arabs circumcised their sons at the age

---

2. J. C. Connell, "Circumcision" in *The New Bible Dictionary* (Grand Rapids: Wm. B. Eerdmans Publishing Co., 1977), 233.

of thirteen because Ishmael, their progenitor, was circumcised at that age. Circumcision is universally practiced by Moslems, not on the authority of the *Koran*, which does not enjoin it, but in the tradition of following the example of their prophet Mohammed.

Female Circumcision?

Strange as it may seem, some cultures actually make it their practice to circumcise girls at the age of puberty. *The World Book* says, "A procedure called *female circumcision* is practiced by many ethnic groups, particularly in Africa and the Middle East. This procedure involves the partial or complete removal of the clitoris, a sensitive part of the female genitals, or the labia, the folds of tissue covering the clitoris. The operation is done for cultural reasons."[3]

It is a very dangerous practice and as one reference work says, "The operation is sometimes attended with grave consequences, hence should be done by surgeons only." Like many other biblical practices, circumcision has been changed by sinful men into something cruel and entirely removed from the original purpose given to it by God.

The Purpose of Circumcision

As we saw above, the Bible says that circumcision was a sign of the covenant that the Lord made with Abraham, the father of the Hebrews. But it was more than that. It has taken medical science four thousand years to discover another reason for the rite of circumcision.

Circumcision and Cancer

In the early 1900s, Dr. Hiram Wineberg of New York's Mount Sinai Hospital, observed that Jewesses were comparatively free from cancer of the cervix, one of the most common cancers in women.

---

3. Martin Weisberg, M. D., Clinical Associate Professor in Obstetrics and Gynecology, Thomas Jefferson University, "Circumcision" in *World Book Deluxe Edition*, Version 4.01, 2000. Distributed on CD by IBM.

Cancer of the cervix comprises twenty-five percent of all cancers in women and eighty percent of all genital cancers.

Following his lead, Dr. Ira Kaplan and his associates at New York's Bellevue Hospital studied their records and were also astonished by the scarcity of cancer of the cervix among Jewish women.

In 1949, the doctors at the Mayo Clinic noted that in 568 consecutive cases of cancer of the cervix not one Jewish woman was among them. Since Jews made up about seven percent of all patients admitted patients admitted to the clinic, there should have been about forty Jewish women with the disease.

In 1954, another survey was done in the city of Boston with 86,214 women. That survey showed that cancer of the cervix among non-Jewish women was nine times more frequent than in Jewish women. Skeptics were still not convinced and thought the findings were due to something else, perhaps diet, food or environment.

Then, a survey was done in India, where food and environmental conditions in many cases were bad. Most of India is divided between Hindu and Moslem practitioners. Moslems practice circumcision; Hindus do not. Authorities were amazed to discover that many more Hindu women had cancer of the cervix than Moslem women. Could this be another reason for God's command to Abraham and all Hebrews to circumcise their male children?

Eighth Day Safest

God told Abraham to circumcise male infants when they were eight days old. Why did God specifically say the *eighth day?* Why not the third, fifth, sixth, tenth, or the twentieth? Medical science confirms that the eighth day of a baby's life is the safest time for a newborn child to undergo an operation. *Why?*

Dr. Emmett Holt and Dr. Rustin McIntosh report that a newborn infant has "peculiar susceptibility to bleeding between day two and day five of its life . . . Hemorrhages at this time, though often inconsequential, are sometimes extensive; they may produce serious damage to internal organs, especially the brain and cause death from shock and exhaustion."

Apparently the tendency to hemorrhage is due to the fact that the bloodclotting element, vitamin K, is not formed in the intestinal tract in normal amounts until the fifth to seventh day of life. Consequently, the first safe day to circumcise a boy would be the eighth day—the very day that the Lord commanded Abraham to circumcise Isaac.

Another element necessary for the clotting of blood is prothrombin. In his book, *Holt's Pediatrics*, Dr. Emmet Holt says that on the third day of a baby's life available prothrombin is only thirty percent of normal. Any operation during that time would predispose a child to serious hemorrhage. On the eighth day, however, the level of prothrombin skyrockets to one hundred ten percent of normal! It then levels off at one hundred percent.

Surely this is another reason to honor God's sovereignty, omniscience, and providence. He and he alone knew these amazing facts about vitamin K and prothrombin four thousand years ago! We commend medical science for its research and the discovery of the information about vitamin K and prothrombin, but Abraham had the right day to circumcise because he believed and obeyed God.

The Importance of Circumcision

Man was responsible for circumcision because it was effective only by the obedience of man, especially the obedience of parents toward their child. Circumcision indicated how much faith parents had in the covenant, providence, and mercy of God. Man was not only responsible for circumcision, but he had to install certain restrictions to ensure its continual practice.

For example, a man could not partake of the Passover, the most important feast in the Jewish economy, unless he had been circumcised. The Bible says that "no uncircumcised person shall eat thereof" (Exodus 12:48). The Jews had a saying, "A circumcised beggar is nearer to God than an uncircumcised king."

Two Outstanding Examples

The Old Testament has two outstanding examples of the importance of circumcision. The Lord almost *killed* his great servant Moses because he had neglected to circumcise his two sons who had been born of Zipporah, his Gentile wife (Exodus 4:24–26).

The other example is the Israelites who, after being delivered from Egyptian slavery, neglected to circumcise their children in the wilderness. For forty years, while they were dying for their unbelief and disobedience at Kadesh Barnea, they did not circumcise their children, the express visible sign of God's covenant with Abraham.

Before their descendants could enter the Promised Land, God told Joshua, "Make thee sharp knives and circumcise the children of Israel" (Joshua 5:2). The Lord gave the reason when he said, "This day have I rolled away the reproach of Egypt from off you. Wherefore the name of the place was called Gilgal [a rolling] unto this day" (Joshua 5:9). It was not just the circumcision of a few babies, but a time-consuming operation on thousands of men as well—all of whom had to remain at Gilgal until they were healed.

Apostolic Explanation

Since the sinless Son of God was taken to the temple when he was eight days old to be circumcised, the rite is seen to be held in high regard. Jesus' circumcision was in obedience to God's covenant with Abraham. How amazing this is in light of these words of Jesus: "Verily, verily, I say unto you, Before Abraham was I am" (John 8:57).

Paul the Apostle gave an enlightening comparison of the physical act of circumcision with the inward experience of faith:

> And he received the sign of circumcision, a seal of the righteousness of the faith which he had yet being uncircumcised: that he might be the father of all them that believe, though they be not circumcised; that righteousness might be imputed unto them also: And the father of circumcision to them who are not of the circumcision only, but who also walk in the steps of that faith of our father Abraham, which he had being yet uncircumcised. (Romans 4:11–12)

A Divine Pledge

Paul was quoting from Genesis 15 and 17, showing that the covenant mentioned in both chapters was one and the same. The main difference between the two chapters is that one contains more of the *divine side* ratifying the covenant. The other contains the *human side* or the keeping of the covenant in obedience to the divine command.

Paul noted that the Bible nowhere says that circumcision was a seal to anyone but Abraham. According to Paul, circumcision was "a seal of the righteousness of the faith which he had yet being uncircumcised." And even in his case it did not communicate any spiritual blessing. It simply confirmed what God had already promised to him.

As a seal from God, circumcision was a divine pledge or guarantee that from Abraham would issue that seed, Jesus Christ, who would bring blessing to all nations. And it promised that they would receive that blessing on the same terms as "justifying righteousness" had become Abraham's—by *faith alone*. Circumcision was not a seal of Abraham's faith, but of the righteousness which, in due time, was to be wrought by the Lord Jesus Christ, the Messiah and Mediator between God and man.

Circumcision was not a memorial of anything which had already been actualized, but an earnest, a guarantee of that which was yet to come in future—namely, of that justifying righteousness which was to be brought in by Christ.

The covenant promised a *numberless* seed to Abraham. Circumcision, as a token of that covenant, must have been a sign of this. But it was not a definite sign to any other, with the exception of Isaac and Jacob to whom the covenant was repeated.

No doubt Israel included married couples who were childless and many like Zelophehad (Numbers 27:1) who had daughters but no sons. Ishmael, who was excluded from it, also had no personal interest in the covenant.

Circumcision Was Compulsory

In addition, circumcision was not submitted to voluntarily nor given with reference to faith. It was compulsory and every male slave bought with money by an Israelite had to be circumcised.

If circumcision sealed nothing to those who received it, except in the case of Abraham, why did God ordain it to be administered to all his male descendants? First, it was the mark God selected to distinguish that people, from whom the Messiah was to come, from all other nations. Second, it served as a continual reminder that the promised seed would spring from Abrahamic stock. Soon after Christ's death, circumcision as a sign disappeared.

The Confusion over Circumcision

Circumcision is just like any of the other symbols, commands, or doctrines that God has given to man. It has been perverted. The only time that Jesus mentioned circumcision in his earthly ministry was in response to the Jews, who were angry with him for healing a man on the Sabbath.

> "If a man," he said, "on a Sabbath day receives circumcision, that the Law of Moses should not be broken; are ye angry with me because I made a man every whit whole on the Sabbath day?" (John 7:23)

Legalists of the Early Church

Recorded in Acts 15, the first church council ever called was over the matter of circumcision. Legalists in the early church said that Gentiles could not be saved unless they were circumcised after the manner of Moses (Acts 15:1). The council was called in Jerusalem to decide the matter. "The Holy Spirit," said Peter, "put no difference between us (Jews) and them (Gentiles) purifying their hearts by faith" (Acts 15:9).

Then James, who seemed to be presiding over the council, said, "Wherefore my sentence is, that we trouble not them, which from the Gentiles are turned to God" (Acts 15:19).

The council then sent a letter to the Gentile Christians in Antioch, which reads in part: "Forasmuch as we have heard that certain which went out from us have troubled you with words, subverting your souls, saying, Ye must be circumcised and keep the law: to whom we gave no such commandment" (Acts 15:24).

That settled the matter as far as trying to make circumcision a requirement for salvation. After two thousand years, however, religions are still trying to do the same thing. But instead of circumcision, they say one must be *baptized* to be saved. This is wrong because the Bible says, "For by grace are ye saved through faith; and that not of yourselves: it is the gift of God: not of works, lest any man should boast" (Ephesians 2:8–9).

Circumcision Not Required for Christians

Under the Old Testament covenant of the law, God required his people to be circumcised; but today, under the New Testament covenant of grace, circumcision is not a requirement for believers in Jesus Christ. Therefore, there must have been a change from the Old Testament to the New Testament. Paul the Apostle explained the change in these words:

> But as God hath distributed to every man, as the Lord hath called every one, so let him walk. And so ordain I in all churches. Is any man called being circumcised? Let him not become uncircumcised. Is any called in uncircumcision? Let him not be circumcised. Circumcision is nothing, and uncircumcision is nothing, but the keeping of the commandments of God. Let every man abide in the same calling wherein he was called. (1 Corinthians 7:17–20)

> For in Jesus Christ neither circumcision availeth anything, nor uncircumcision; but faith which worketh by love. . . . And I, brethren, if I yet preach circumcision, why do I yet suffer persecution? Then is the offence of the cross ceased. (Galatians 5:6,11)

Circumcision and Infant Baptism

The once-for-all offering of Jesus Christ supplanted the Old Testament sacrifices. The Melchisedec high priesthood of the Lord Jesus Christ superseded the Aaronic priesthood of Israel. Therefore, spiritual circumcision has superseded physical circumcision. Here is how Paul explained this:

> And ye are complete in him, which is the head of all principality and power: In whom also ye are circumcised with the circumcision made without hands, in putting off the body of the sins of the flesh by the circumcision of Christ: Buried with him in baptism, wherein also ye are risen with him through the faith of the operation of God, who hath raised him from the dead. (Colossians 2:10–12)

Those who believe and teach the system of doctrine known as "covenant theology"[4] say that these verses teach that New Testament baptism replaces Old Testament circumcision. The brilliant Protestant Reformer and theologian John Calvin also used Colossians 2:11–12 in an attempt to prove that infant baptism was the successor of Old Testament circumcision. He wrote:

> Hence it is incontrovertible that baptism has been substituted for circumcision, and performs the same office. . . . In explanation of his sentiment he (Paul) immediately adds, that we are "buried with him in baptism." What do these words mean, but just that the truth and completion of baptism is the truth and completion of circumcision, since they represent one thing? For his object is to show that baptism is the same thing to Christians that circumcision formerly was to the Jews.[5]

A careful examination of Colossians 2:11–12, however, shows that Calvin's exegesis is in error. There, through Paul the Apostle, the

---

4. If you would like to know more about the errors of covenant theology, see George Bowman's book, *Covenant Theology and the Word of God.*

5. John Calvin, *Institutes of the Christian Religion* (Christian Library on CD), 1473 & 1479.

Holy Spirit says that New Testament circumcision is "made without hands," so it can't mean baptism. After all, it is impossible to administer either circumcision or baptism without hands. He also said it was the "operation of God."

In Romans 4, Paul said that circumcision was a seal of the righteousness of faith, but not once in the New Testament does it say *baptism* is the seal of the New Covenant. In fact, Paul wrote that the Holy Spirit was the seal of the New Covenant. Speaking to Christians, he said that after they had believed in Christ they "were sealed with that Holy Spirit of promise" (Ephesians 1:13).

A Presbyterian minister said he firmly believed that New Testament baptism took the place of Old Testament circumcision. When he was reminded of the fact that the Jews only circumcised their male children and was asked why he baptized girl babies, he said, "I never thought of that before."

There is not one line or one sentence in the Bible that says that baptism takes the place of circumcision. To attach tradition, assumption, presuppositions, or human reasoning to an ordinance of the church is simply heresy. History reveals that the Protestant Reformers carried this false teaching over from the Roman Catholic Church instead of discarding it like they did with other Roman Catholic errors.

THE SYMBOLISM OF CIRCUMCISION

The Circumcision of Christ

Since Paul the Apostle says in Colossians that believers are circumcised with the circumcision of Christ made without hands, one might ask, "What is the circumcision of Christ?" This question should not be too difficult to answer because in the Old Testament Moses spoke of *spiritual circumcision*.

"And the LORD thy God," he said, "will circumcise thine heart, and the heart of thy seed, to love the LORD thy God with all thine heart, and with all thy soul, that thou mayest live" (Deuteronomy 30:6).

Circumcision of the Old Testament was physical—a type or symbol that pointed to Christ and the circumcision (or "tearing away of the flesh") he performs by his Holy Spirit on the carnal heart. The *New English Bible* translates Colossians 2:11 to read: "In him also you were circumcised, not in a physical sense, but by being divested of the lower nature; this is Christ's way of circumcision." In other writings of Paul the Holy Spirit enlightens us with this truth repeatedly in several ways:

> For he is not a Jew, which is one outwardly; neither is that circumcision, which is outward in the flesh: But he is a Jew, which is one inwardly; and circumcision is that of the heart, in the spirit, and not in the letter; whose praise is not of men, but of God. (Romans 2:28–29)

> Is he the God of the Jews only? Is he not also of the Gentiles? Yes, of the Gentiles also: Seeing it is one God, which shall justify the circumcision by faith, and uncircumcision through faith. (Romans 3:29–30)

> For we are the circumcision, which worship God in the spirit, and rejoice in Christ Jesus, and have no confidence in the flesh. (Philippians 3:3)

God required physical circumcision of the Jew. He had to be circumcised to be a citizen of Israel and a recipient of Old Covenant blessings. In a similar way, the Lord said it was absolutely imperative that one receive the circumcision of Christ to become a citizen of the kingdom of God, a recipient of New Covenant blessings, and a member of his royal family.

That circumcision is regeneration or the *new birth,* an independent, sovereign work of the Holy Spirit. The new birth gives the sinner the desire, the ability, and the will to repent of his sins and believe in Jesus Christ as his Lord and Saviour.

Christ's way of circumcision, then, enables the believer to be triumphant over his old sinful, self-centered nature with its lusts, passions and self-interests. To be rid of these unprofitable attitudes is to a man's great advantage. Modern psychiatrists recognize these as the causes or aggravations of the kinds of stress that can lead to more serious physical problems. Dr. Hans Selye, for example, wrote a book with this title: *Stress: The Cause of All Disease.*

Circumcision of the Spirit

It seems that physical circumcision prevents two kinds of fatal cancer, but Christ's spiritual circumcision of our evil, Adamic nature (or the new birth) prevents a far greater number of diseases. As we have already seen, circumcision of the body foreshadowed the circumcision of the spirit. That is why physical circumcision is not required of Christians. Is it not amazing that both the literal act and the *type* in many cases prevent deadly disease?

Failure to observe the symbol or rite of circumcision made the Jew a spiritual outcast. In light of this, we can understand why God says that one cannot belong to him unless he has been circumcised with Christ's spiritual circumcision. Once that takes place, the Christian has new power over his own sinful desires. "And they that are Christ's have crucified the flesh (sinful nature) with the affections and lusts" (Galatians 5:24).

Only when one has received this divine surgery can he enjoy the promises of his heavenly Father. It is a wonderful work of God that Paul called "a new creation" when he wrote these words: "For in Christ Jesus neither circumcision availeth anything, nor uncircumcision, but a new creation. And as many as walk according to this rule, peace be on them, and mercy, and upon the Israel of God" (Galatians 5:15–16).

The True Israel Of God

To show how circumcision has been abolished and how dangerous it is to add circumcision to one's faith as a means of getting right with God, Paul wrote these words: "Stand fast therefore in the liberty wherewith Christ hath made us free, and be not entangled again with the yoke of bondage. Behold, I Paul say unto you, that if ye be circumcised, Christ shall profit you nothing" (Galatians 5:1–2).

One of the great truths of Scripture is that the true Israel of God is the church or the Body of Jesus Christ, made up of all those in heaven and on earth who are saved by grace alone . . . through faith alone . . . in Christ alone.

May the Lord use this study of circumcision to encourage you to manifest in your life the fact of your spiritual circumcision, your new spiritual birth, which enabled you to repent and to believe in Jesus Christ to the praise of his glorious grace.

> Thank you for that operation
> that was never made by hand;
> Thank you, Lord, for circumcision
> on my soul, the inward man.
> (Author unknown)

CHAPTER TWO

The Reluctant Missionary

My wife and I once heard an Independent Baptist Minister in Florida say that under the Old Testament Law there was no concern for missions and no missionary was ever sent forth. But he was mistaken because the Old Testament contains an account of one of the most successful foreign missionary expeditions in the world.

Mercy and Judgment

The missionary was Jonah, who lived in the time of King Jeroboam II of Israel (782 B.C.), and the mission field was Nineveh, the capital city of Assyria. Under Jonah's preaching more than 120,000 residents there repented of their sins and were delivered from destruction.

Jonah's story can be found in the prophecy of Jonah, an Old Testament book of only four chapters and forty-eight verses that can be read in about fifteen minutes. Jonah and Nahum are the only two books in the Bible that end with questions, and both questions are about the people in Nineveh. Jonah ends with a question of mercy, but Nahum ends with a question of judgment.

In Jonah's day God had mercy on Nineveh and the people repented. In the days of Nahum, one hundred fifty years or about four generations later, God destroyed the city because of the people's wicked rejection of the Lord and his truth. The history of Nineveh contains important lessons for our generation. God is a God of mercy and justice, but when men spurn his mercy and laws by their wicked ways, they bring his judgment upon them. "It is a fearful thing to fall into the hands of the living God" (Hebrews 10:31).

The Sign of Jonah

When most Christians think of the book of Jonah they think of his amazing experiences. But neither they nor Jonah himself is the great theme of this little book. The great theme of the book of Jonah is an unusual topic: God's concern for 120,000 persons who were not his chosen people, the Israelites. They were Gentiles or pagan idolaters!

Why did God choose to include this little book in his inspired Word, the Bible? The answer comes from the Lord Jesus Christ, who said that Jonah was a sign to the Ninevites and he, likewise, would be a sign to his generation. Our Lord spoke thus about Jonah in answer to the scribes and Pharisees who had said to him, "Master, we would see a sign from thee."

> An evil and adulterous generation seeketh after a sign; and there shall no sign be given to it, but the sign of the prophet Jonah: for as Jonah was three days and nights in the whale's belly' so shall the Son of man be three days and three nights in the heart of the earth. The men of Nineveh shall rise in judgment with this generation, and shall condemn it: because they repented at the preaching of Jonah; and, behold, a greater than Jonah is here. (Matthew 12:38–41)

Jokes are often made about Jonah and the whale, and unbelievers like to mock and laugh at those who believe his story. But, as Christians, we have to believe Jonah's story because Jesus, the God-man, authenticated it by saying that it had happened. Having established its authenticity, let us make a further study of this short book to grasp four important realities: Jonah's statement of faith, Jonah's sovereign resurrection, Jonah's sign or message, and Jonah's God.

Jonah's Statement of Faith

The Storm at Sea

Jonah's story begins with the Lord commanding him to go to Nineveh, the capitol city of Assyria, and preach against its wickedness. Jonah, however, was a bigoted Jew who hated all Gentiles, so he rebelled against the commandment and decided to run from the Presence of the Lord.

He went to Joppa (present day Jaffa), a seaport about thirty-five miles from Jerusalem. There he found a ship getting ready to sail to Tarshish, the likely ancient location of which was Spain—more than two thousand miles away.

When the ship was well out to sea on the Mediterranean, Jonah went down into the hold to sleep. Suddenly, a great wind rose up that caused a raging storm. It must have been an unusual storm, because the captain and his crew were afraid their ship would be smashed to pieces by the mountainous waves. Each member of the crew cried out to his pagan god. In an attempt to lighten the ship and save their own lives, they threw the cargo overboard.

Remembering his passenger, the Captain went to Jonah and woke him up saying, "What meanest thou O sleeper? Arise and call upon thy God, if so be that God will think upon us, that we perish not" (Jonah 1:6).

How a Statement of Faith Should Begin

The sailors decided to cast lots in order to learn for whose cause the storm had come upon them. When they did so the lot fell upon Jonah. "Tell us, we pray thee," they said to him, "for whose cause this evil is upon us; what is thine occupation? And whence comest thou? What is thy country? And of what people art thou?" (Jonah 1:6–9)

"I am an Hebrew," said Jonah: "and I fear the Lord, the God of heaven, who made the sea and the dry land." In his response to the crew Jonah gave a statement of his faith with words similar to those written by Moses in Genesis 1:1: "In the beginning God created the heaven and the earth."

This is how a biblical statement of faith should begin because if one genuinely believes those first words of Genesis, he will never have any difficulty believing the rest of the Bible. For example, David's creed was also the same: "Happy is he that hath the God of Jacob for his help, whose hope is in the Lord his God: which made heaven, and earth, the sea, and all that therein is: which keepeth truth for ever" (Psalm 146:5–6).

The truth of creation by a sovereign God was also included in statements of faith made by Paul the Apostle, and John, the beloved disciple. When the pagan Gentiles thought Paul and Barnabas were gods and were ready to *worship them,* Paul and Barnabas responded by tearing their clothes and running in among the Gentiles.

"Why do ye these things?" they shouted at the pagans, "We also are men of like passions with you, and preach unto you that ye should turn from these vanities unto the living God, which made heaven, and earth, and the sea, and all things that are therein" (Acts 14:15).

When Paul was invited to speak to Greek philosophers on Mars Hill in Athens, he gave a similar statement of faith. "God that made the world and all things therein," he said, "seeing he is Lord of heaven and earth, dwelleth not in temples made with hands; neither is worshiped with men's hands, as though he needed any thing, seeing he giveth to all life, and breath, and all things" (Acts 17:24–25).

John followed the same creation theme in his Gospel. Speaking of Jesus Christ, the Word as God, he said, "All things were made by him; and without him was not any thing made that was made" (John 1:3).

The Supreme Truth

God's creation is a good place to start a statement of faith. Moses, Jonah, David, Paul, and John began with creation because the supreme truth of the universe is the reality of the sovereign God as the Creator of all things. Paul emphasized the importance of this when he wrote these poignant words: "The wrath of God is revealed from heaven against all ungodliness and unrighteousness of men, who hold [or, *suppress*] the truth in unrighteousness" (Romans 1:18).

That God as Creator of all things *is* the Supreme Truth has been proved and is being proved by the complex and intricate elements in his created order of things. In spite of a plethora of evidences for God and creation, pagan unbelievers "changed the truth of God into a lie, and worshiped and served the creature more than the Creator who is blessed forever" (Romans 1:25).

While Paul wrote this passage about the pagan gentiles of his day, the principles it contains apply to our time as well. Modern unbelievers are doing the same thing that the Gentiles of the first century did. Their guilt, however, is greater because they have at their disposal much more information about God and his creation than was available two thousand years ago. Their judgment, too, will be worse than that of the first century Gentiles.

A Strong Delusion

Although Paul lived in the first century and wrote about his contemporaries, here is a passage he wrote that is appropriate for today's society: ". . . they received not the love of the truth, that they might be saved. And for this cause God shall send them strong delusion, that they should believe a lie." The original reads "the lie" not "a lie," because it is likely Paul was speaking of the lie that Satan used in the Garden of Eden.

Satan, whom Christ described as "the father of lies," told Eve that she would not surely die if she ate of the forbidden fruit in violation of God's specific command not to do so. Then he said, "For God doth know that in the day ye shall eat thereof: then shall your eyes be opened, and ye shall be as gods [or as God], knowing good and evil" (Genesis 3:5).

With these words Satan tempted Eve with an offer of autonomy or *self-law*. Eve was seduced into believing that if she and Adam could be "as God," then they would be autonomous—a law unto themselves—and have no need of God, who had made them and had given them life.

The Lie in Evolution

This is the very principle of erroneous thinking that produced the theory of evolution—that the universe came into existence *by chance,* without the need for a Creator. This lie, then, has led to the rejection of God, the exaltation of man, and the promotion of vain philosophies like humanism, existentialism, modernism, and atheism.

The lie of the evolutionary philosophy has spread like an epidemic across the world. In his book, *The Bible has the Answer,* Dr. Henry Morris, a creation scientist, explains:

> The evolutionary philosophy is the intellectual basis of all the anti-Christian, and anti-God, systems that have plagued mankind for centuries. It served Hitler as the rationale for Nazism and Marx as the supposed scientific basis for communism. It is the basis of the various modern methods of psychology and sociology that treat man merely as a higher animal and which have led to the misnamed "new morality" and ethical relativism. Its whole effect on the world and mankind has been harmful and degrading. Jesus said; "A good tree cannot bring forth evil fruit" (Matthew 7:18). The evil fruit of the evolutionary philosophy is evidence enough of its ultimate origin in Satan's age-long rebellion against his Creator.[1]

This lie shows up in almost every college and university. For example, a student in a West Virginia college took courses in science

---

1. Henry M. Morris, *The Bible Has the Answer* (Nutley, New Jersey: The Craig Press, 1973), 80.

that included instruction in the theory of evolution. When he came to take the final examination for one of the courses, he found it contained a question about the origin of the earth. After answering the question, the young man added this note: "This is the answer you taught and want, but I do not believe it. I believe in God and in the record he gave in the Bible."

The professor, in this case, was an honest and fair man and gave the student an "A" on the examination and also an "A" for the course. This isn't always the case, however, for young people in secular public education.

Jonathan Edwards, one of the most brilliant theologians of all the settlers of early America, had this to say about creation: "Among the many acts of gratitude we owe to God, it may be accounted one to study and contemplate the perfection and beauties of his work of creation. Every new discovery must necessarily raise in us a fresh sense of the greatness, wisdom, and power of God."

How wonderful it would be if scientists of our day would embrace that statement by Edwards!

JONAH'S SOVEREIGN RESURRECTION

"Cast me into the sea!"

After he made his statement of faith, Jonah also told the captain of the ship and his fellow sailors that he had disobeyed God and was fleeing from his Presence. This made the men exceedingly afraid (Jonah 1:10–14).

"Why hast thou done this?" they asked him, in fear of their lives. "What shall we do unto thee, that the sea may be calm unto us?"

"Take me up," said Jonah, "and cast me forth into the sea; so shall the sea be calm unto you: for I know that for my sake this great tempest is upon you."

Not wanting to throw their passenger overboard, the men rowed hard to bring their ship to land. But it was no use. The wind grew stronger, the waves mounted higher, threatening to capsize the vessel. This moved the men to pray to the God of Jonah. "We beseech thee, O Lord, they prayed, "let us not perish for this man's life, and lay not upon us innocent blood: for thou, O Lord, hast done as it pleased thee."

When they finished praying, they picked Jonah up and cast him headlong into the raging waves crashing around the ship. Immediately the wind stopped blowing, the storm subsided, and the waters of the Mediterranean Sea became calm.

Prayer in a Fish's Belly

Beneath dark waters, however, something supernatural was going on. God had prepared a great fish in such a way that it was able to swallow Jonah down into its stomach without doing his physical body any harm, "And Jonah," says the Bible, "was in the belly of the fish three days and three nights" (Matthew 12:40).

During the time Jonah was in the belly of the great fish, he prayed to the Lord. His prayer takes up nearly all eight verses of Jonah, Chapter Two. Indeed, the prophet knew that he had disobeyed the Lord and had foolishly tried to flee the Presence of He who is omnipresent, omniscient, and omnipotent. So, in Jonah's prayer, he acknowledged the sovereignty of God in having him cast into the sea and swallowed by the great fish.

Salvation Is by Grace Alone.

Knowing that he was at fault he said, "I will look again toward thy holy temple . . . I will sacrifice unto thee with the voice of thanksgiving. I will pay that I have vowed. Salvation is of the Lord" (Jonah 2:9). At last, Jonah was ready to change directions and do what the Lord had asked him to do. The Lord responded to his prayer by speaking to the fish, causing it to spew Jonah out upon dry land.

When Jonah said, "Salvation is of the Lord," he likely meant that, if he was going to be delivered from the belly of the fish, God would have to do it. But there is an important principle here that we would do well to think about: God was not only the deliverer of Jonah from his predicament, but the sinner's salvation and deliverer from sin.

"Salvation is of the Lord," or, "Salvation by divine grace alone!" was the battle cry of the Protestant Reformers more than two thousand years after Jonah lived. Their doctrines were called the "doctrines of sovereign grace" because they believed that men were saved by sovereign grace alone through the gift of faith in Jesus Christ alone. They believed that the salvation of a sinner contained not one microscopic element of human effort. It was *all* of God.

Modern Changes in Evangelism

Over the centuries since then, things have changed. Instead of the doctrines of sovereign grace in salvation, many preachers teach that God cannot save a sinner unless the sinner allows him to do so. You'll hear these preachers say, "God wants to save you, but you won't let him."

In almost every evangelistic crusade, the preacher tells people to *do* something in order to be saved. The truth that *God* does the saving without the help of man is rejected. Consequently, people have the idea that they must go forward, make a decision, "let go and let God," give God a chance, or pray by repeating words given to them by the preacher.

If today's evangelical preachers and evangelists would just believe that "salvation is of the Lord" and only of the Lord, it would revolutionize their preaching. It would honor and glorify God instead of using words and methods that honor and glorify man.

Jonah Points to the Believer's Two Resurrections

Besides pointing to the doctrines of sovereign grace, the story of Jonah is a type of the death, burial, and resurrection of Jesus Christ. For as Jonah was three days and three nights in the whale's belly," said Jesus; "so shall the Son of man be three days and three nights in the heart of the earth" (Matthew 12:40).

The deliverance of Jonah was *a resurrection* performed by the sovereign God from what would otherwise have been certain death. Similarly, God raised Jesus from the grave.

There is another lesson here. Jonah's experience also points to the believer's two resurrections: his spiritual resurrection or new birth and his future resurrection, which will come when he is raised from death by God to a new life in heaven.

"Verily, verily I say unto you," said Christ, "The hour is coming, and now is, when the dead shall hear the voice of the Son of God: and they that hear shall live" (John 5:25). These words of Christ speak of our spiritual resurrection or *the new birth.*

In the same Chapter, verse 29, Jesus describes what many believe to be our future resurrection. "All that are in the graves," he says, "shall hear his voice, and shall come forth: they that have done good, unto the resurrection of life; and they that have done evil, unto the resurrection of damnation."

Jonah's Sign or Message

We last saw Jonah on the beach after the whale had spewed him out of his stomach. Now, the Lord repeats his command for Jonah to go to Nineveh and preach the message of warning that he had given him. At last, Jonah obeys the Lord and heads in the right direction.

A Tremendous Response

The city of Nineveh was so large that it took three days to walk through it. When Jonah had walked into the city for one day, he began to cry out, "Yet forty days, and Nineveh shall be overthrown!" (Jonah 3:4). The response was tremendous.

The king laid aside his royal robes, dressed himself in sackcloth, and sat in ashes—signifying his own repentance. Then he commanded all the people of Nineveh to do the same, to refrain from eating and drinking, and even to prevent their livestock from feeding or drinking water. It was a time for national repentance and the king sent out this proclamation to the people: "Let them turn every one from his evil way, and from the violence that is in their hands. Who can tell if God will turn and repent, and turn away from his fierce anger, that we perish not?" (Jonah 3:8–9).

When God saw that they were sincere and that they turned from their evil ways, he did not overthrow the city as he had said he would. Jesus' words made it clear that the *sign of Jonah* pointed to both his resurrection and judgment. That evil generation of the first century, he said, would receive no sign but the judgment sign of Jonah.

"The men of Nineveh," he said, "shall rise up in the judgment with this generation, and shall condemn it" (Matthew 12:41).

A Major Emphasis

The men of that generation were to be judged and condemned because they refused to repent, as the men of Nineveh had done, and believe in Christ. Clearly, a major emphasis in the *sign of Jonah* is that God is going to judge and condemn all those who refuse to repent of their sins and believe in Jesus Christ and in his redemptive purpose for coming to the earth.

This message needs to be preached today. Many preachers never mention the subject of God's certain judgment and condemnation of unrepentant sinners. If sinners are not made aware of the certain judgment of God upon them for their wickedness, what would be the sense of preaching the Gospel to them? Did not Jesus say, "Except ye repent, ye shall all likewise perish" (Luke 13:3)?

Jonah's God of Mercy

Jonah must be the strangest missionary we have ever heard or read about! He preached a message of judgment to a foreign city filled with wicked and violent people who were so vicious they had become notorious for their cruelty. In spite of their severe and offensive lives of sin, over 120,000 Gentile people in Nineveh believed a Jewish missionary and repented of their sins.

How did Jonah respond to this great revival? Expecting to see the judgment of God fall upon the wicked people of that city, he got furiously angry when God chose not to destroy them! The Bible says that God's mercy to Nineveh "displeased Jonah exceedingly, and he was very angry."

Jonah then prayed unto the Lord this unusual prayer:

> I pray thee, 0 Lord, was not this my saying, when I was yet in my country? Therefore I fled before *unto* Tarshish: for I knew that thou art a gracious God, and merciful, slow to anger, and of great kindness, and repenteth thee of the evil [or judgment]. Therefore now, 0 Lord, take, I beseech thee, my life from me; for it is better for me to die than to live. (Jonah 4:2–3)

God responded to Jonah from the heart of a loving Father: "Then said the Lord, 'Doest thou well to be angry?'" Isn't it wonderful that God does not answer our selfish and often quite *stupid* prayers? God had sent a storm, caused the sailors on the ship to cast Jonah overboard, and prepared a great fish to swallow his errant prophet. He also protected him in the fish's stomach for three days and three nights, then commanded the fish to spew him out, unhurt, onto dry land.

After Jonah preached God's message, more than 120,000 people had repented and turned from their wicked ways. Yet, in response to all these supernatural events, Jonah's response was to get angry and plead to die!

How can we explain Jonah's strange reaction? Well, first of all, it is likely that Jonah, as a Jewish bigot, had no love for Gentiles. Further, he was likely embarrassed because he had told the people that their city would be overthrown in forty days and it wasn't going to happen because, instead of judgment, God had mercy on the people in Nineveh.

Jonah was so angry he left town and went to a rise of ground just east of Nineveh, where he had a good view of the city. There he sat down, waiting to see what would become of the city. While Jonah sat there, the Lord prepared a gourd as a shade over Jonah's head to deliver him from his grief.

"And Jonah was exceedingly glad because of the gourd." The next morning, however, "God prepared a worm that caused the gourd to wither." Then God prepared a vehement east wind and the sun beat upon Jonah's head until he fainted and wanted to die. "It is better," he said, "for me to die than to live."

"Doest thou well," the Lord asked Jonah, "to be angry for the gourd?"

"I do well," he answered, "to be angry, even unto death." Then said the Lord, "Thou hast had pity on the gourd, for the which thou hast not labored, neither madest it to grow; which came up in a night, and perished in a night: And should not I spare Nineveh, that great city, wherein are more than six score thousand persons that cannot discern between their right hand and their left hand; and also much cattle" (Jonah 4:9–11)?

In spite of Jonah's bad attitude (reluctant, disobedient, self-pitying, bigoted, and so angry he wanted to die), and erroneous response to the Nineveh revival, he was right in his characterization of God. He had said that God was gracious. We who have been saved by his grace should rejoice in that quality of God's character. Listen to Paul as he revels in the grace of God:

> Having predestinated us unto the adoption of children by Jesus Christ to himself; according to the good pleasure of his will, to the praise of the glory of his grace, wherein he hath made us accepted in the beloved. In whom we have redemption through his blood, even the forgiveness of sins, according to the riches of his grace. (Ephesians 1:5–7)

Jonah had said rightly that God was merciful. Here is Peter extolling that wonderful quality of God's character:

> Blessed be the God and Father of our Lord Jesus Christ, which according to his abundant mercy hath begotten us again unto a lively [or living] hope by the resurrection of Jesus Christ from the dead, to an inheritance incorruptible and undefiled, and that fadeth not away, reserved in heaven for you. (1 Peter 1:3–4)

Jonah also said that God was slow to anger, and of great kindness, and that He would not punish even wicked men and women so long as they repented. How grateful and filled with joy we should be that the character of our God is what Jonah said it was!

Because he is slow to anger, of great kindness, and has a concern for sinners, we can urge men and women still in their sins to repent and to receive Jesus Christ as their Lord and Saviour. We can tell them that God will not punish them if they repent and believe the Gospel of God's redemptive grace in the crucified and risen Christ.

Therefore, let us go forth as missionaries, not reluctant as Jonah was, but with much prayer and preparation and with earnest anticipation of what God will do where the Gospel of his grace is preached to sinners according to his Word!

> Preach the Word, preach the Word,
> Tell the Gospel you have heard;
> Be instant in and out of season,
> For the hope within you give a reason.

CHAPTER THREE

A Jewel Box of Truth

Does your mother, your wife, your sister, your fiancé possess a jewel box? Some verses in the Bible could rightly be described as *jewel boxes* in themselves. A jewel box is used to keep precious possessions, such as diamonds, rubies, pearls, rings, cameo brooches, and necklaces, safely stored. The Bible, too, safely stores many passages that are filled with precious jewels of truth.

All Are Not Equally Profitable

"All scripture," said Paul, "is given by inspiration of God, and is profitable for doctrine, for reproof, for correction, for instruction in righteousness" (2 Timothy 3:16). Every page of the Bible, therefore, is inspired by God, but all passages are not *equally* profitable. Some passages are more enlightening than others.

There is no comparison, for example, between an Old Testament genealogy table and the New Testament record of Christ's miracles. Neither is there comparison between 1 Chronicles 6 and John 6, between Ezra 2 and Ephesians 2, between Genesis 36 and Isaiah or Jeremiah or Ezekiel 36. The passages in the Gospel of John, the Epistle to the Ephesians, the Prophecy of Isaiah, the Prophecy of Jeremiah and the Prophecy of Ezekiel reveal *more* divine truth, speak with *greater* clarity and force, inspire and promise more than those in 1 Chronicles, Genesis, or Ezra.

A Citadel of Grace Doctrines

The sixth chapter of John's Gospel is one of the greatest chapters in all the Bible. It contains more verses and is the longest chapter John wrote. It also contains these interesting items: the miracles of Christ feeding the five thousand and walking on the Sea of Galilee; Christ's discourse on the bread, in which he said, "I am the Bread of Life"—one of his great "I am" declarations; Peter's twofold declaration that Christ alone had the words of eternal life and that he was the Son of the living God; and Christ's prophetic word to his disciples that, ". . . one of you is a devil" (John 6:70).

John, Chapter 6 is also a citadel for the doctrines of sovereign grace and the discipleship that is based on those doctrines. Hence, those who hold to the Arminian School of doctrine rarely preach on John, Chapter 6. It contains verses that plainly refute the man-centered position that one is saved by the exercise of his own free will.

A Text on Which to Hang One's Soul

John 6 contains several verses that could be described as "jewel boxes of truth," but my purpose is to display the jewels of truth in John 6:37, those in which the Lord Jesus is reported as saying, "All that the Father giveth me shall come to me; and him that cometh to me I will in no wise cast out." Here is an unusual topic: a scriptural jewel box containing brilliant diamonds of eternal truth, cultured pearls of great price, and the transparent blue sapphire of certain assurance.

Someone has said that this text, with all its jewels of truth, is "the best Word in the Bible." John Bunyan, author of *Pilgrim's Progress*, said, "It is a text for a man to hang his soul upon since it speaks, not of the people who come, but of the person to whom they come . . . his ability, his willingness, and his love to those who are afar off and to them who are nigh."

When Charles Spurgeon preached on John 6:37 he titled his sermon "High Doctrine and Broad Doctrine." He said that people like to call the first part of the text high doctrine or Calvinistic doctrine, but the latter part they say is broad doctrine because they come to this evangelistic appeal as a statement without limitation of any kind, with the idea that the free grace of God is open to the free will of man so that whosoever pleases may come and be sure that he will not be refused. He also said, "We have no permission to pare down either sentence, nor is there the slightest need to do so."

The precious jewels in this jewel box of truth may be described as follows: Salvation is in a person. Some will come to Christ. Those who come were given by God to his Son. And only those who come will be saved.

Salvation Is in a Person

Correcting Mistakes Many Make

Theologians would agree that the emphasis in this jewel box of truth is on the four personal pronouns, "me, me, me," and "I," all of which speak of Christ. In this passage, it seems to be shouting that salvation is in a person. That being true, it's clear that salvation is not in a church, a religious rite, good ideals, a good moral character, or even sound doctrine. Salvation is in none other than the person, Jesus Christ, the sinless Son of God, who could look his enemies in the face and ask, "Which of you finds me guilty of sin?" He was the spotless, atoning Lamb slain on the Cross of Calvary!

This is so important that I would like to correct the mistakes many make with regard to the grounds of their personal salvation. The fact is, one could be baptized in the biblical way—by immersion—and still be lost. Although some churches teach that one must be baptized in order to be saved, no one is saved by baptism. Baptism is a personal confession of one's identification with the death, the burial, and the Resurrection of Christ, but it has nothing to do with salvation, which is by sovereign grace alone.

In one church I saw these words from Matthew 3:15 displayed over the baptistery: "Suffer it to be so now: for it becometh us to fulfill all righteousness." Those words of Christ spoken to John the Baptist just before he baptized Christ are beautiful words of Scripture, but they had to do with Christ, not the baptism of redeemed sinners. Such an inscription could leave the impression that one getting baptized is *fulfilling all righteousness,* which is not true. One could regularly participate in the Lord's Supper and be lost. One can make a profession of faith by going forward in church or at an evangelistic crusade and yet not be saved. A man could be an intellectual theologian, know all the doctrines that Calvin taught, and be spiritually lost.

He Argued Religion in Beer Joints

When I attended seminary I was pastor of a church in which a man, who was not a member, was more interested in the Bible than many of the members. He wrote away for all of the literature offered on the radio by M.R. DeHaan and could argue about religion day and night with anyone. In fact, he used to go to the local beer joints on his way home from work to drink beer and argue about religion with his drinking partners.

One day he had a heart attack and died suddenly. He left his widow and friends doubting whether he had been redeemed. But one cannot go to the Saviour with true repentance and genuine, God-given faith and be lost! And that is exactly what Jesus said in John 6:37.

Some Will Come to Jesus

In John 6:36 Jesus said to those in his audience, "But I say unto you, that ye also have seen me, and believe not." Did their refusal to believe dishearten or discourage Christ? Far from it—because he knew from all eternity that some were going to believe.

God's Purpose Will Stand

What a lesson that is for pastors, missionaries, and evangelists! One's message may be slighted by the crowd; he may become unpopular; many he ministers to may reject his claims that Jesus Christ is the Son of God and the Redeemer of sinners. Some, however, will believe! One may labor in the ministry for a lifetime and see only a handful saved. Yet, God's purpose will stand, His will be done.

After writing about false teachers who had overthrown the faith of some, Paul the Apostle said, "Nevertheless the foundation of God standeth sure, having this seal, the Lord knoweth them that are his; and let everyone that nameth the name of Christ depart from iniquity" (2 Timothy 2:19).

Many times it can be discouraging to live a good Christian life and be a faithful witness for Christ while seeing few visible fruits, yet the results can be genuinely successful. Why? Because God knows those who are his. Prior to the flood, Noah preached for some hundred and twenty years, but only his wife, his sons, and their wives were saved from the flood by entering the ark.

John the Baptist was the harbinger of Jesus the Messiah and saw huge crowds attend his preaching. Yet he became discouraged after his arrest and imprisonment. So discouraged, in fact, that he sent some of his disciples to Christ with this question: "Art thou he that should come, or do we look for another?" (Matthew 11:3).

Even Christ himself must have felt somewhat discouraged in his humanity after many of his disciples deserted him. Nearing the final days of his earthly ministry, he turned to his twelve disciples and asked, poignantly, "Will ye also go away?" Unbelief itself is no sign that God's plan to redeem a people for himself is failing.

"For what if some did not believe?" asked Paul. "Shall their unbelief make the faith [or faithfulness] of God without effect?" (Romans 3:3)

Vessels of Mercy

Later in the same epistle Paul, in his unusual style of answering questions with questions, said, "What if God, willing to show his wrath and to make his power known, endured with much longsuffering the vessels of wrath fitted to destruction: that he might make known the riches of his glory on the victory vessels of mercy, which he had afore prepared unto glory?" (Romans 9:22–23).

When a sarcastic unbeliever tells you he does not believe the Bible, think of God's unchangeable purposes and say, "Do you really think that your unbelief can cancel God's everlasting truth?"

The prophet Isaiah spoke of unbelief when he began the 53rd chapter with a question that sounded almost like a lament: "Who hath believed our report?" he asked. Did that question mean that Isaiah was discouraged? On the contrary. Ten verses later he made a wonderful statement of consolation and confirmation. He said that the Lord "shall see the travail of his soul, and shall be satisfied: by his knowledge shall my righteous servant justify many; for he shall bear their iniquities." These words are prophetic of what Christ said in John 6:37: "All that the Father giveth me shall come to me."

Who Then Can Be Saved?

We should never try to interpret the success or failure of God's plans by our circumstances, experiences, emotions, or even the results of our ministry. For example, God told Jeremiah and Ezekiel to preach to the nation of Israel. Yet before they began to preach the Lord told them that the people would not believe.

In the light of all this it would be quite natural to ask the same question asked of Christ by the disciples: "Who then can be saved?"

"The things that are impossible with men," said Christ, "are possible with God."

The Scripture does not teach that *all* are going to be saved when the Gospel is preached. But it does say that after Paul preached in Antioch of Pisidia, "as many as were ordained to eternal life believed" (Acts 13:48).

After Paul was mocked by blaspheming Jews in Corinth and left the synagogue, it would appear that he had every right to be discouraged. He then went next door to the house of Justus, where he spoke to Crispus the chief ruler of the synagogue and to several Corinthians. Crispus and many of the Corinthians believed and were baptized.

To further encourage Paul, the Lord spoke to him in a vision and said, "Be not afraid, but speak, and hold not thy peace, for I am with thee and no man shall set upon thee to hurt thee, for I have much people in this city" (Acts 18:9–10).

A Source of Encouragement

When Paul and Silas went to Philippi they found a gathering of women praying. The record does not say that all the women believed, but that the Lord opened the heart of Lydia, one of the women, so that she attended unto the things spoken by Paul. Clearly, it was the Lord who opened her heart to believe and submit to baptism.

That incident should be a source of great encouragement to pastors, evangelists, missionaries, and those who witness one-on-one for Christ. The Lord opens the hearts of those he has chosen and given to Christ. Not long after the Lord saved Lydia, he opened the heart of a jailor who had taken Paul and Silas and had thrust them into an inner cell and fastened their feet in stocks. The Lord used an earthquake in the prison area to send the jailor trembling to Paul and Silas to ask them, "What must I do to be saved?" Paul's answer led to the man's entire family believing in Christ and being baptized.

Those Who Come Were Given by God to His Son

As a former pastor, I am amazed at how many ministers seem to be ignorant about the subject of who is going to be saved. John 6:37 is not an isolated passage about men and women getting saved because God the Father had given them to his Son, Jesus Christ. The same truth appears seven times in John 17, the high priestly prayer of Christ to his Father just prior to his Crucifixion. This is such a wonderful chapter that John Knox, the Scottish Reformer had it read to him continually in the last days of his life.

God Saves the Unexpected

Modern evangelists keep saying that the heathen people of the world are crying out for God, just waiting for missionaries to come to them with the Gospel. But it just isn't so. All men of all races are in darkness because they were born with a sinful nature inherited from Adam. The Lord Jesus confirmed this when he said, "And this is the condemnation, that light has come into the world, and men loved darkness rather than light, because their deeds were evil" (John 3:19).

The Lord not only said who was going to be saved; he gave examples of some he did save. Many of them would be the last ones *we* would expect to be saved. They were not righteous persons or churchgoers or moral persons, but the opposite.

For example, he saved Zachaeus, a cheating tax collector who, after conversion, admitted that he had defrauded the people. He also saved the demoniac of Gadara, who ran naked among the graves and could not be restrained even with chains. He saved the woman at the well, who had five husbands and was then living with a man who was not her husband.

These people were not dragged, forced, or pulled on a leash. They had been given to Christ by the Father, and they went to Christ because the Father had drawn them—"No man can come unto me," said Jesus, "except the Father which hath sent me draw him: and I will raise him up at the last day" (John 6:44).

Man's Total Inability

Notice that this verse does not say, "No man *will* come to me," but, "no man *can* come to me," which means no one has the ability to come. It is impossible for one to come to Jesus until God the Spirit implants within him the seed of regeneration or new spiritual birth.

That is why Jesus said to Nicodemus, "Except a man be born again he cannot see (or enter) the kingdom of God" (John 3:3,5).

Only Those Who Come Will Be Saved

Distorted Views of Predestination

Some allow the second part of John 6:37 to steer them away from the doctrine of predestination or to give a distorted view of that biblical doctrine. For example, Spurgeon told the story of a man with an unpaid debt. When the creditor came to collect, the debtor said to him, "I understand you are a Calvinist. Do you think I am predestined to pay this debt?"

"I do not think," said the creditor, "that the doctrine of predestination has anything to do with this transaction. You owe me so many pounds and if you do not pay me you are a thief and can be prosecuted for it."

In the early days of American history a certain clergyman was a strong believer in God's providence and in predestination. Since he had to go through a long stretch of woods to get to church, he always carried his gun with him to protect himself and his family from possible attack by Indians. One morning, an unbeliever who never attended church was sitting on the porch of his cabin as the clergyman and his family walked by.

"Hey, preacher," he yelled, "if what is going to be is going to be, why carry a gun?"

"I never know," said the clergyman, "when it is time for a certain Indian to take his last breath."

I use these illustrations because some Christians who are strong in Calvinistic beliefs can forget the meaning of the last part of John 6:37, the *broad* part of the verse as Spurgeon called it. "And him that cometh to me," said Jesus, "I will in no wise cast out."

Beware of Confusion

We should be careful not to confuse election with the action of salvation. Election took place in eternity before creation. Paul said that God "hath chosen us in him [Christ] before the foundation of the world" (Ephesians 1:4). But salvation takes place in real time. Speaking to the Philippian jailor, Paul said, "Believe on the Lord Jesus Christ and thou shalt be saved" (Acts 16:31).

All sinners do not come to Christ in the same way. Some come immediately, without hesitation. Others come haltingly. And some, like John Bunyan, will be weeks, maybe months, under conviction of their sins before they come. Regardless of how they come, however, they do get saved. Both the snail and the turtle made it into the ark and were saved from the flood.

No Need for Doubts about Election

Perhaps some reading these lines have doubts about their salvation because they wonder if they have been elected. Let me ask you this: Have you come to Christ? If you have, never forget that Christ said that *whosoever* came to him he would in no way cast out. If you have come to Jesus, sincerely believing in him as your Lord and Saviour, then you are one of that untold number whom God the Father has given to his Son Jesus Christ. For this, there are neither requirements nor pedigrees nor limits. Jesus said, "All that the Father giveth me shall come to me; and him that cometh to me I will in no wise cast out."

It is important for us to realize that there is no set time in life when an elect person will come to Christ. Statistics show that most Christians are saved early in life. But others, like the dying thief on the Cross, are saved just before they die.

Many pastors could give you examples of men and women coming to Christ late in life. A woman in the church I formerly pastored in Charleston, West Virginia, came to Christ the first time she attended services. She was well over seventy years of age! She submitted to baptism and manifested her salvation by never missing the Sunday services or the Wednesday night meeting for as long as I knew her.

What Others Have Said

As we come to the close of this chapter, let's look at what others have said about John 6:37. "This scripture," said John Bunyan, "did most sweetly visit my soul. Oh, the comfort I have had from the words 'in no wise,' for they are saying, by no means, for no thing, whatever he has done." Bunyan needed those words because before his conversion to Christ he had been a foul-mouthed tinker.

When the English Bishop Butler was dying, he complained that his sickness and the delirium from his sickness coming off and on were robbing him of the assurance of his salvation.

"My Lord," said a chaplain standing nearby, "you forget that the Lord Jesus is a Saviour."

"True," said Butler, "but how shall I know he is a Saviour for me?"

"My Lord, it is written, 'him that cometh to me I will in no wise cast out.'"

"True, I have read that scripture a thousand times," said Butler, "but never knew its true value until right now that you have pointed it out at my dying."

What a marvelous book is the Word of God! In John 6:37, Jesus went from a vast number, the plural noun "all" to personal salvation, using the personal, singular pronoun "him" in one sentence. There is a blessed certainty of salvation for any person who comes to Jesus.

For example, Peter denied Christ with curses, but he was not cast out. Thomas doubted the report of Christ's Resurrection, but he was not rejected. Lot and David were guilty of sexual immorality, but they were not cast out because salvation is of the Lord.

"All that the Father giveth me," said Jesus, "shall come to me; and him that cometh to me shall in no wise be cast out." Hymn writer Joseph Humphrey knew this truth and wrote these lines of invitation to those who knew they were guilty of sinning against God:

> Come, guilty souls, and flee away
> To Christ, and heal your wounds;
> This is the welcome Gospel day
> Wherein free grace abounds.

Unusual Topics

God loved the church, and gave his Son
To drink the cup of wrath;
And Jesus says he'll cast out none
That come to him by faith.

CHAPTER FOUR

The Power of
Predestinating Purpose

Horace Greeley, a controversial American journalist and political leader of the Nineteenth Century, said he thought that Abraham Lincoln was a great president to guide the nation in a time of peace. He did not, however, think so highly of him as a leader of the American people in time of war.

His Time Had Not Yet Come

Present at Lincoln's inauguration, Greeley wrote these interesting words: "I sat just behind Lincoln as he read his Inaugural Address on a bright, warm, still March day, expecting to hear its delivery arrested by the crack of a rifle aimed at his heart. But it pleased God to postpone the deed, though there were forty times the more reason for shooting him in 1861 as there was in 1865, and at least forty times as many intent on killing him or having him killed. No shot was fired, however, for his hour had not yet come."

In his words, ". . . his hour had not yet come," Horace Greeley gave his philosophy of history and of life. Lincoln was not assassinated in 1861 because his hour had not yet come. The implication of all this is that when Lincoln *was* assassinated his hour *had* come. The same holds true for Stonewall Jackson, who was mistakenly shot by his own troops. John F. Kennedy was assassinated when his hour had come, as were his brother Robert Kennedy and Martin Luther King, Jr. What can we learn from this?

"To everything there is a season."

"That," says someone, "sounds like predestination." It not only sounds like predestination—it is predestination!

I call the Doctrine of Predestination an unusual topic because it seems to me that a lot of people believe in predestination but many will not admit it. Written by Solomon to show that life is meaningless apart from God, the book of Ecclesiastes teaches predestination in Chapters 1:9 and 3:1–2:

> The thing that hath been,
> it is that which shall be;
> And that which is done
> is that which shall be done . . .
> To every thing there is a season,
> and a time to every purpose under heaven:
> A time to be born,
> and a time to die.

Many a soldier in time of war has written home to say, "If I am killed in battle, it will be for no other reason than that my hour has come." Another soldier might put it this way: "If I get killed in this war, it will because the bullet with my name on it has finally found its target." General George Patton risked his life many times under fire, he said, because he believed that during those times his hour had not yet come.

Predestination Is Not Fatalism

Soldiers who talk like that usually believe in fatalism, but it is not fatalism: it is predestination. There is a tremendous difference between predestination and fatalism. Theologian Dr. Loraine Boettner explains that difference:

Fatalism holds that all events come to pass through the working of a blind, unintelligent, impersonal, non-moral force which cannot be distinguished from physical necessity, and which carries us helplessly within its grasp as a mighty river carries a piece of wood. Predestination teaches that from all eternity God has had one unified plan or purpose which he is bringing to perfection through this world order of events.[1]

People in all walks of life die when their hour has come because their time was in God's hands and the death of every human being has been predetermined as part of the eternal purposes of God.

The Power of God

This chapter is about three words we would do well to define before we go on. Those three words are: power, predestination and purpose. *The power of God* is another way of saying that God is omnipotent. Theologian Augustus H. Strong defined "omnipotence" as "the power of God to do all things which are objects of power, whether with or without the use of means."

Puritan Stephen Charnock said, "The power of God is that ability and strength whereby he can bring to pass whatsoever he pleases, whatsoever his infinite wisdom may direct, and whatsoever the infinite purity of his will may resolve."

Predestination: To Determine Beforehand

The word *predestinate* appears six times in the New Testament and means "to determine beforehand, to foreordain." In his book, *Absolute Predestination*, Jerome Zanchius makes this statement: "Predestination is the bond which connects and keeps together the whole Christian system, which without predestination is like a system of sand, ever ready to fall to pieces. It is the cement which holds the institution together; nay, it is the very soul that animates the whole frame. It is

---

1. Dr. Loraine Boettner, *The Reformed Doctrine of Predestination* (Phillipsburg: The Presbyterian and Reformed Publishing Company, 1981), 205.

so blended and interwoven with the entire scheme of Gospel doctrine that when predestination is excluded, the Gospel bleeds to death."

Many have neglected, berated, ignored or criticized this very important doctrine of the Christian faith because, they say, "It is too difficult to understand." Ephesians 1:11, however, gives an excellent description of predestination. Though *The Living Bible* is not a translation but a paraphrase with human interpolations, author Ken Taylor was right on target about predestination in his paraphrase of Ephesians 1:11:

> Moreover, because of what Christ has done we have become gifts to God that he delights in, for as part of God's sovereign plan we were chosen from the beginning to be his, and all things happen just as he decided long ago.

That definition of predestination seems to be as simple as one can put into layman's language an understanding of the term.

God's Eternal Purpose

Many people seem to have no lasting purpose in life. They go from one job to another. They wait for the weekend to live it up. But they are not really living because without a lasting purpose they merely exist. How different it was with the Lord Jesus Christ! He had a purpose for coming to earth as the virgin-born babe of Bethlehem. He had a purpose for living his near 33 years. And he had a purpose for allowing men to crucify him on a Roman cross. After describing the apostate Pharisees as thieves whose purpose was to steal, to kill, and to destroy people, he said, "I am come that they might have life, and that they might have it more abundantly" (John 10:10).

The Bible says emphatically that God, who sent Christ to earth, has an eternal purpose. The *purpose* of God is his fixed determination to bring a result to pass. What he has purposed he will never change. Thus, the person who wants to understand the Word of God must study his purposes and his fixed determination.

The Bible does not say that God works according to his judgment. He does not have to judge, as we do, whether this or that will be best. He purposes or "worketh all things after the counsel of his own will" (Ephesians 1:11). His particular purposes are revealed in the Bible, and one of those purposes is recorded in these words by Paul the Apostle from Ephesians 1:9–10:

> Having made known to us the mystery of his will, according to his good pleasure which he hath purposed in himself: that in the dispensation of the fullness of times he might gather together in one all things in Christ, both which are in heaven, and which are on earth: even in him.

Nothing Is Left to Chance

God always works according to a definite plan. Nothing is left to haphazardness. For instance, God's plan for the salvation of his people in any age is always by propitiatory sacrifice, or substitutionary atonement, always without any variation. Also on the part of the redeemed there is always needed faith to rely on the sacrifice—a faith supernaturally given by God. It is a great trust for us, who are not able to save ourselves, to rely for eternity on a sacrifice that someone else provides to make us safe forever.

The saints of the Bible—from Abel, the son of Adam, to John, the author of the final book of the New Testament, relied on a sacrifice. And their reliance was faith—faith in Jesus Christ as Lord and Saviour. This divine plan of salvation for sinners stands in opposition to human religions that teach their devotees to *do* something, whereas God's plan says it has all been done. When Jesus was dying on the Cross as God's appointed sacrifice for sin, he cried, "It is finished." That is why every believer in him loves to sing the classic chorus:

> Jesus paid it all,
> All to him I owe;
> Sin had left a crimson stain;
> He washed it white as snow.

We have looked at the definitions of divine power, predestination, and purpose. If you would like to increase your knowledge of the power of predestinating purpose, join me as we take the rest of this chapter to look at three important and practical aspects of that power: first, its extent; second, its effectiveness; and third, its essence.

The Extent of the Power of Predestinating Purpose

Divine Providence

We often hear of people whose lives, by a kind providence, were spared in an accident. By not taking a certain train or plane or ship that met with disaster, some were saved from injury or death. In some unaccountable way they narrowly missed being the target for the arrow of death. But what about those who did take the train or plane or ship and were killed? Should we exclude providence in their deaths?

John Bunyan tells of an experience that provides an answer. Drafted as a soldier to fight in the Civil War in England, he was to take part in the siege of Leicester. As he was ready to leave for the battle area, another man asked to go in his place. Writing about it, John Bunyan said, "He took my place; and coming to the siege, as he stood sentinel, he was shot in the head by a musket bullet and died." The same providence that saved John Bunyan to write *Pilgrim's Progress* was also present in the death of his substitute.

Power Over All Flesh

It is true that the emphasis in the predestinating purpose of God is on the elect. And whether we call them the elect, believers, the redeemed, saved ones, sheep, or God's people, we have to acknowledge that the power of God's purpose extends to all persons and all things related to his plan to redeem a people for himself.

Jesus Christ makes this point in his high priestly prayer. "As thou hast given him power over all flesh, that he should give eternal life to as many as thou hast given him" (John 17:2). Notice that Christ was given power over all flesh! That power was rightfully his because he was born of a woman and took part in our humanity. He "was made flesh and dwelt among us" (John 1:14).

The author of Hebrews also said, "Forasmuch then as the children are partakers of flesh and blood, he also himself likewise took part of the same" (Hebrews 2:14). He not only lived in a human body, but he died as a human being. "Christ also hath once suffered for sins, the just for the unjust," said Peter, "that he might bring us to God, being put to death in the flesh, but quickened by the Spirit" (1 Peter 3:18).

Infinite, Limitless Power

The extent of Christ's power appears in his great commission to his disciples. "All power," he said, "is given unto me in heaven and in earth" (Matthew 28:18). Think of the extent of his power: it was *all* power in heaven and in earth. It was supreme power over all creation.

The Bible also says that Christ "through death destroyed him that had the power of death, that is, the devil; and delivered them who through fear of death were all their lifetime subject to bondage" (Hebrews 2:14).

Here is one of the main reasons for Christ's Incarnation, but we'll never see that verse on a Christmas card. His almighty power goes even beyond this world and death. Paul the Apostle referred to Christ's divine power in Ephesians 1:19–21:

> And what is the exceeding greatness of his power to us-ward who believe, according to the working of his mighty power, which he wrought in Christ, when he raised him from the dead, and set him at his own right hand in the heavenly places, far above all principality, and power, and might, and dominion, and every name that is named, not only in this world, but also in that which is to come.

That is infinite, limitless power! How delightful it is to dwell upon the royal attributes of our blessed Christ! What encouragement our faith finds in the contemplation; what ground of hope and blissful expectation! All power in heaven and earth—his! All power over the enemy of our souls—his! All power over that which is within us and contrary to us—his! All at his absolute disposal and the controlling power that was bestowed upon him for this end and object: that nothing might hinder him, or interfere with him in the discharge of his office—"that he should give eternal life to as many as God hath given him" (John 17:2).

The realms of nature, the boundless stores of grace, the fullness of glory, and power over all flesh are lodged in the mediatory hands of the Lord Jesus Christ. Knowing this, we can understand why the apostle Paul, sensing the tremendous security of the believer, closes one of the greatest chapters in all the Bible with these words:

> For I am persuaded, that neither death, nor life, nor angels, nor principalities, nor powers, nor things present, nor things to come, Nor height, nor depth, nor any other creature, shall be able to separate us from the love of God, which is in Christ Jesus our Lord. (Romans 8:38–39)

THE EFFECTIVENESS OF THE POWER OF PREDESTINATING PURPOSE

He Prayed About a Key

Though the Bible clearly states that Christ has power over all flesh, many question his interest and control over the minute, everyday things that happen in their lives. Yet his control over those small things has brought about great changes in history. Charles Spurgeon saw the truth of this. Speaking to Spurgeon of another Christian, a man said, "He is an odd fellow: he prayed about a key the other day."

"Why not pray about a key?" asked Spurgeon. "Why not pray about a pin? Sometimes it may be as important to pray about a pin as it is to pray about a kingdom. Little things are often linchpins of great events." History contains many recorded events that prove the absolute truth of what Spurgeon said here.

Columbus and Calvin

For example, the story is told of how Christopher Columbus, leading his young son by the hand, was making his way on foot back to Italy, disheartened and discouraged because he could not find a sponsor for his desired journey of discovery. One day he stopped at a convent and asked for a drink of water. The monk who gave him the drink and listened to his story was the same person who later intervened for him with Queen Isabella of Spain. Out of that seemingly insignificant request for a drink of water came the discovery of America!

A road blocked due to war between France and Italy caused John Calvin, who was on his way to a quiet life of study in Italy, to detour through Geneva, Switzerland. There in October, 1536, he met the French Reformer, Guillaume Farel who, with fiery eloquence, demanded that Calvin stay in Geneva to help with the Protestant Reformation instead of retreating from society. What a great significance there was for the cause of truth in *that* detour!

Napoleon and Lincoln

Another event that changed the course of history happened to Napoleon Bonaparte just prior to the Battle of Waterloo. On the eve of June 18, 1815, the rain in Belgium was so heavy and the roads so soft that Napoleon, who had won his battles with artillery, could not get his guns into position until eleven A.M. in the morning.

Had it not rained, he could have had his guns up and operating by seven A.M. instead of eleven and the battle would have been won by two P.M.—three hours before Blucher and his Prussian force came to the aid of Wellington and affected the victory for Wellington's mixed allied army. "A cloud traversing the sky out of season," said a historian, "sufficed to make a world crumble."

Another seemingly insignificant event happened to young Abraham Lincoln. Rummaging in a barrel of rubbish someone had left in his store, he came upon a copy *of Commentaries on the Laws of England* by Sir William Blackstone, the Solicitor General to Queen Victoria. As he read it, Lincoln's ambitions and desires were awakened to study law and to serve his country. That so-called "chance" discovery inspired him to become a president who played a great part in American history.

Whitefield and Moses

The son of an impoverished English innkeeper in Gloucestershire, a young man could not get along with his brother's wife. This led him to give up his job at the Bell Inn and go to Bristol. From there, step by step, he went to Oxford, where the Lord called him to faith in Christ and to service in the ministry.

He soon became one of the world's greatest preachers and was used to kindle the Eighteenth Century spiritual revival that swept through England, Scotland, Wales, and the English colonies in America. His name: George Whitefield, and the revival of which he was such an important part was called The Great Awakening.

"The difference I had with my brother's wife," he said, "was God's way of forcing me out of the public drawing of wine for drunkards to drawing water out of the wells of salvation for the refreshment of his spiritual Israel."

A biblical example of how God uses small things to initiate great events is a baby's cry at the Nile River bank, which was heard by Pharaoh's daughter. She adopted the child she found floating in a basket, crying, and raised him as her own son. His name was Moses, and when he grew up God used him to deliver the Israelites from slavery in Egypt. This is yet another example of how God works all things after the counsel of his own will.

A Soft Pillow for a Tired Heart

Yes, *things* as well as persons are under the power of predestinating purpose. "And we know," said Paul, "that all things work together for good to them that love God, to them who are the called according to his purpose" (Romans 8:28). The well-known American evangelist R. A. Torrey called this verse "a soft pillow for a tired heart."

The phrase "all things" means both dark and bright things, both happy and sad things, and both sweet and bitter things. It also means both times of prosperity and times of adversity.

When we reflect upon the innumerable and infinitesimal things that God works together for good in the lives of the saints, we must rejoice in the effectiveness of his power to accomplish his purpose. About a thousand years before Paul, David spoke about the same truth in a prayer to the Lord. "All things," he said, "are thy servants" (Psalm 119:91).

How sad that so many professing Christians, including church ministers, fail to believe that not just things but *people* are under God's predestinating purpose! It is also sad and obstructive to spiritual growth that a large number of Christians do not believe these words of Jesus: "All that the Father giveth me shall come to me," and "No man can come to me, except the Father which hath sent me draw him" (John 6:37, 44).

THE ESSENCE OF THE POWER OF PREDESTINATING PURPOSE

The Bottom Line

A popular saying in our day is: "That's the bottom line." It means, "After stripping away the veneer this is the gist or essence of the matter, this is the key value." The *bottom line* or essence of the *power of predestinating purpose* is this: God is really God and his Word and power can do anything. To have faith in God is to believe this to be true. A major problem throughout the history of Christianity has been the tendency of believers to question this eternal truth. Even the disciples of Christ had to be rebuked and reprimanded for their doubts and for their smallness of faith.

When the disciples were frightened by a storm on the Sea of Galilee, Jesus said to them, "Why are ye fearful, O ye of little faith?" (Matthew 8:26). To Peter, who tried to walk on water and began to sink, Jesus rescued him and said, "O thou of little faith, wherefore didst thou doubt?" (Matthew 14:31). When his disciples were concerned because they had forgotten to bring bread with them to Magdala, Jesus, who had recently used five loaves and two fish to feed five thousand people, said, "O ye of little faith, why reason ye among yourselves, because ye have brought no bread?" (Matthew 16:8).

Jesus also said that if his disciples had faith as small as a grain of mustard seed they could remove obstacles, which he likened to mountains. "Nothing," he said, "shall be impossible to you" (Matthew 17:20). He also said that if his disciples had faith and did not doubt that all things whatever they asked in prayer, believing, they would receive (Matthew 21:20–22). O how little we know of the power of genuine faith in God!

Developing Faith

The Bible says, "Let us lay aside every weight and the sin that doth so easily beset us" (Hebrews 12:1). I believe that *besetting sin* is unbelief. Faith does not come to us full blown. It must be nurtured and developed by church attendance, Bible study, Christian fellowship, and prayer. Let us make up our minds to believe in the predestinating power of God's purpose and trust him to work all things together for our good because, by his grace, we love him and are *the called according to his purpose.*

An example of this kind of faith is seen in the old Negro spiritual entitled, "Joshua at the Battle of Jericho." Some of the lyric reads, "You have heard about your men of Gideon; You have heard about your men of Saul . . ." The words then go on to extol the faith and feat of Joshua when the walls of Jericho "came tumbling down" and the Israelites captured the enemy's stronghold after marching around the city seven times.

The Shunammite Woman

Another wonderful example of great faith in God was that of the Shunammite woman in the days of Elisha. Knowing that Elisha was a man of God, she arranged a chamber room for him in to sleep whenever he passed her way. She also fed him. When Elisha asked what he could do for *her* as a reward for her kind hospitality, his servant Gehazi spoke up and said, "Verily she hath no child and her husband is old" (2 Kings 4:14).

Knowing the very great value that people in those times placed on children, Elisha called the woman to him and said, "About this season according to the time of life, thou shalt embrace a son."

"Nay, my lord, thou man of God," she said, "do not lie unto thine handmaid" (2 Kings 4:16). The thought of having a son was just too wonderful for her to imagine!

Sure enough the woman gave birth to a son as Elisha had said she would. Some years later, when the child was grown and working with his father in the field, he suffered a sunstroke and this happiness turned to instant horror.

"It is well with the child."

A servant carried the unconscious boy to his mother, who sat him on her knees. At noon that day, the youth died and his mother took him up and laid him on Elisha's bed. Shutting the door behind her, she went out and sent word to her husband saying, "Send me, I pray thee, one of the young men, and one of the asses, that I may run to the man of God, and come again" (2 Kings 4:22).

When the ass was saddled she said to her servant, "Drive, and go forward; slack not thy riding for me, except I bid thee" (v 24).

When Elisha, who was in Mount Carmel, saw her, he sent a servant to greet and ask her, "Is it well with thee? Is it well with thy husband? Is it well with the child?"

"It is well," she answered (2 Kings 4:26).

What an amazing thing to say with a dead son lying on a bed back at her house! I don't think there would be one in a million persons who would have answered Elisha's questions like that. How could she do it? The answer, I think, is that she knew her son was a gift from God because of Elisha's faith and prayers. Also she did not think that God had given her a son for a few years just to tantalize her. She believed that God could use Elisha to bring her son back from the dead; she had *faith* that this was true.

At that time in history only one other person had ever been raised from the dead. Some years before, God had used Elijah to raise the son of the widow who lived in Zarephath of Zidon, but there is no record that the Shunammite woman knew about that miracle.

More Faith than Mary and Martha

When Elisha got to the house, the Lord used him to raise the son to life. The woman was rewarded for her trust in God's purpose for her life and the life of her son. Some time later, Elisha warned her of a coming seven-year famine, so she fled to the land of the Philistines. After the famine, when she returned to Israel, the king restored all her lands and possessions because he believed the account he had heard of Elisha raising her son from the dead.

The Shunammite woman had more faith than Mary and Martha, who lost their brother Lazarus when he died. She had more faith than the thousands who had seen the miracles of Jesus with their own eyes and heard his words.

A Sea Captain Learns about Faith

Some may say, "She was a Bible character. We do not have people with that kind of trust and belief about God in this day and age." But this is not true. There are many not recorded in the Bible who were also men of great faith.

For example, here is the true story of how a sea captain learned about genuine faith in the Lord. Charles Inglis, a noted British evangelist, said that when he first went to America he crossed the Atlantic in a steam ship whose captain was one of the most devoted Christians he had ever met. When the ship was off the banks of Newfoundland the captain turned to the evangelist and told this story:

> Mr. Inglis, the last time I crossed here, months ago, one of the most extraordinary things happened that completely changed and revolutionized the whole of my Christian life forever. We had a man on board, George Mueller of Bristol. Up to that time I was one of your ordinary, professing Christians, but his belief and actions changed my shallow faith.

> We were in a dense fog and I had been on the bridge for twenty-two hours and never left it. I was startled by someone tapping me on the shoulder. It was George Mueller. "Captain," he said, "I have come to tell you that I must be in Quebec on Saturday afternoon."

> It was Wednesday. "It is impossible," I said.

> "Very well," said Mueller, "if your ship cannot take me God will find other means to take me. I have never broken an engagement in fifty seven years."

> "I would willingly help you," I said, "but how can I? Look at this fog. I am helpless."

> "Let us go down to the chart room," said Mueller, "and pray."

> I looked at this so-called man of God and said to myself, *What lunatic asylum could this man have come from? I had never heard of such a thing.* "Mr. Mueller," I said, "do you know how dense this fog is?"

> "No," he said. "My eye is not on the density of the fog, but on the living God who controls every circumstance of life, especially my life."

When we got down to the chart room he got down on his knees and prayed one of the most simple prayers that would suit a Sunday school class of children if the children were not eight or nine years old. The burden of his prayer was something like this:

"O Lord, if it is consistent with thy will, please remove this fog in five minutes. Thou knowest the engagement thou didst make for me in Quebec for Saturday. I believe it is thy will."

When he finished I was going to pray, but he put his hand on my shoulder and told me not to pray. "First," he said, "you do not believe he will answer. Second, I believe he has and there is no need whatever to pray about it. Captain, I have known my Lord for fifty-seven years and there has never been a day that I have failed to get an audience with the King."

In five minutes or less the dense fog had vanished.

God's Word Abides Forever

George Washington prayed at Valley Forge. Stonewall Jackson prayed about the minute things of life. George Mueller prayed for a dense fog to vanish in five minutes. These are only a few examples of thousands like them who have been men of great faith in the power of the predestinating purpose of God. They believed the truth of these words of the Lord spoken through his prophet: "I am God and there is none else; I am God and there is none like me. Declaring the end from the beginning, and from ancient times the things that are not yet done, saying. My counsel shall stand, and I will do all my pleasure" (Isaiah 46:9–10).

The Protestant Reformer Martin Luther believed in God like that and God used him mightily in his spiritual battles with the apostate papacy and the Roman Catholic Church. Here is one of his poems:

The Power of Predestinating Purpose

For feelings come and feelings go,
And feelings are deceiving;
My warrant is the Word of God;
Naught else is worth believing.

Though all my heart should feel condemned
For want of some sweet token,
I know one greater than my heart,
Whose Word cannot be broken.

I'll trust in God's unchanging Word
Till soul and body sever;
The words of men shall pass away;
God's Word abides forever.

CHAPTER FIVE

Rebels and Election

During the American Civil War the eleven Southern states called themselves a *confederacy*. Those in the northern states did not always call a Southern soldier a Confederate soldier. Many times they labeled him a rebel or "Johnny Reb," a term used in derision. There is, however, a big difference between a confederate and a rebel.

A confederate is a member of a confederacy, which is "a union of states or people for a common purpose." But a rebel is "a person who openly resists authority or opposes any control," and to rebel is "to oppose any authority or government by force." While the word "confederate" has some respect about it, the noun "rebel" has a bad connotation.

Moses and the Three Reasons

The word *rebel* is also a biblical word and appears in the statement made by Moses that kept himself and Aaron out of the Promised Land of Canaan. "Hear ye, rebels," he said to the Israelites, "must we fetch you water out of this rock?" (Numbers 20:10) The book of Psalms says that the Israelites angered Moses, "at the waters of strife, so that it went ill with Moses for their sakes: Because they provoked his spirit, so that he spake unadvisedly with his lips" (Psalm 106:32–33).

This does not mean that Moses was kept out of Canaan for using the word *rebels* because the emphasis for wrongdoing was not on the word. There are three reasons that Moses was kept out of the Promised Land. First, he was told to speak to the rock, not to the people. Second, he used the personal pronoun "we" usurping God's power and authority. And third, he struck the rock twice, destroying the type of Christ the Rock, who only needed to give himself once at Calvary as a sacrifice for the sins of his people.

Who Are God's Elect?

Moses was not the only one to call the Israelites rebels. God also called them rebels in Numbers 17:10, and again in Ezekiel 20:38. It is interesting to notice that God called them rebels after the gainsaying of Korah and the rebellion of Dathan and Abiram and after God had punished the Israelites with a plague that killed 14,700 of them, which indicates that they were still rebels after those events.

Some ask, "Why did God call his elect people rebels?" But that poses the question, "Who are the elect people of God?" I have included election as an unusual topic because many fundamentalists and dispensationalists hold to a misconception that the Jews are God's elect people. That is a misconception. *Why?*

Paul the Apostle said, "For they are not all Israel, which are of Israel: Neither, because they are the seed of Abraham, are they all children: but, In Isaac shall thy seed be called. That is, they which are the children of the flesh, these are not the children of God: but the children of the promise are counted for the seed" (Romans 9:6–8).

Paul also said, "But with many of them God was not well pleased; for they were overthrown m the wilderness. . . . Neither murmur ye, as some of them murmured, and were destroyed of the destroyer" (1 Corinthians 10:5,10).

The position of the Israelites was described by Moses when he said, "For thou art an holy people unto the LORD thy God: the LORD thy God hath chosen thee to be a special people unto himself above all people that are upon the face of the earth. The LORD did not set his love upon you, nor choose you, because ye were more in number than any people; for ye were the fewest of all people" (Deuteronomy 7:6–7).

An Unscriptural View

Some think that these verses include not only all the Jews who came out Egypt, but all the Jews living today. But that is an unscriptural view. In Romans 9–11, Paul shows that God had elected certain ones within his special people of Israel. The nation of Israel was chosen by God and marked out and distinguished from all other races, but only some of the people in that nation were of the elect whom God had chosen for salvation.

Many of the Israelites were rebels and many within the professing Christian church are rebels. The elect have been targeted by God's redemptive mercy and it was his prerogative and his alone to choose those of the Israelites who were to receive his mercy, grace, and compassion (Exodus 33:19). Some 1500 years later, Paul made a similar statement: "So then," he said, "it is not of him that willeth, nor of him that runneth, but of God that sheweth mercy" (Romans 9:16).

Christ Preached Election

A big surprise to many is the fact that God permitted that rebellion and fault-finding among his ancient Hebrew people so that *elect Gentiles* might be saved. Paul explained this when he wrote:

What if God, willing to shew his wrath, and to make his power known, endured with much longsuffering the vessels of wrath fitted to destruction: And that he might make known the riches of his glory on the vessels of mercy, which he had afore prepared unto glory. Even us, whom he hath called, not of the Jews only, but also of the Gentiles? (Romans 9:22–24)

77

Although it didn't suit the rebels, the Lord Jesus Christ did not shun to declare the truth about election. What a change there would be in our churches if today's ministers would emulate his example! Why should all of us who are in the Lord's work preach and teach the doctrine of election? You can enjoy a satisfactory answer to that question by learning all you can about these four reasons for preaching the doctrine of election: 1) Election is a biblical truth; 2) Election has meaning; 3) Election is not controversial; and, 4) Election has great value.

Election Is a Biblical Truth

Even Some Christians Oppose Election

The Bible says that every believer is saved because of God's electing grace. "Even so then at this present time also," wrote Paul, "there is a remnant according to the election of grace. And if by grace, then is it no more of works: otherwise grace is no more grace. But if it be of works, then it is no more grace: otherwise work is no more work" (Romans 11:5–6).

The only reason anyone believes in election is that he finds it in the Bible, the inspired Word of God. The natural man could never have conceived of such a doctrine because it is contrary to his way of thinking and to the wishes of his heart. The old sinful nature of man has such influence that even some Christians oppose this doctrine. Ordinarily it is only after various struggles under the working of the Holy Spirit of God that one is able to receive it.

The Bible Emphasizes Election

If the Bible was a work of man alone it never would have contained the doctrine of election because men are too averse to such a thought to give it expression, much less to give it the prominence it has in the Bible. To get rid of election in the Bible one would have to get rid of the Bible itself.

The question is not what do men and women think about election, but what does Scripture teach? The Bible makes election prominent;

it makes election basic to the entire scheme of grace. It puts election as the supreme law, the underlying principle of the Gospel, in which all things have their existence in harmony.

Nehemiah said that God had chosen Abram and given him the name Abraham. In 1 Chronicles, King David said that God had chosen him and his son, Solomon. He also repeatedly referred to God's chosen in the Psalms he wrote.

The Order Is Significant

Though Jesus and Paul were the eminent teachers of election in the New Testament, all the other writers wrote about it as well. Speaking to his disciples, Jesus said, "Ye have not chosen me, but I have chosen you" (John 15:16).

Jesus also said, "Many are called but few are chosen" (Matthew 22:14). He also spoke of God avenging his own elect people, of God giving him those he called *his sheep,* whom he said would come to him. "And him that cometh to me" said Jesus, "I will in no wise cast out" (John 6:37).

The order here is significant: God gives men to Christ before they come to him; they come because they have been given to him; and, having come, they will surely remain in him.

Paul Preached Election

Paul followed Christ in his teaching of election. To the Romans he spoke of those "whom God did predestinate," of which he said, "them he also called." And he also asked this rhetorical question: "Who shall lay anything to the charge of God's elect?"

Writing to the saints in Ephesus, he said they were chosen from before the foundation of the world. He told the believers in Philippi, "To you it is given in behalf of Christ to believe." And he called the Colossian saints "the elect of God" (Ephesians 1:4; Philippians 1:29; Colossians 3:12).

Paul reminded those in the church of Thessalonica that "God hath not appointed us to wrath but to obtain salvation." When he wrote to his fellow ministers, he also wrote about election. To Timothy he spoke of God, "who hath saved us and called us with an holy calling, not according to our works but according to his own purpose and grace, which was given us in Christ Jesus before the world [or before time] began." To Titus, he said that he [Paul] was "an apostle of Jesus Christ, according to the faith of God's elect" (2 Tim. 1:9; Titus 1:1).

Easy to Understand, Hard to Believe

It is obvious that election is a biblical doctrine. If one requires more convincing, he should read with an open mind Ephesians Chapter One and Romans Chapter Nine. In spite of these clear passages on election, some still say, "I simply cannot understand the doctrine of election." Why is this?

In most cases those who make that statement really mean, "I do not want to believe the doctrine of election." Election is not difficult to understand, but for some it is difficult to embrace. They have no trouble understanding the words *choose* and *elect* when it comes to other things. It should not be difficult to understand the time texts that say men were elected before they had done any good or evil or before the foundation of the world. In this regard, we should all pay attention to these lines by the great poet and novelist Sir Walter Scott:

> Within this awful volume lies
> The mystery of mysteries:
> Happiest they of human race
> To whom their God has given grace
> To read, to fear, to hope, to pray,
> To lift the latch, to force the way;
> But better had they ne'er been born,
> Who read to doubt, or read to scorn.

Election Has Meaning

Election Gives God All the Glory

Election means choice and *to elect* means to choose. Election, then, is the absolute choice by God Almighty of those who were selected to be saved—a choice he made before he created the earth. This, of course, gives God all the glory for the salvation of sinners, glory which rightly belongs to him.

All glory belongs to God because, as the prophet Jonah said, "Salvation is of the Lord." Whether we are preachers, seminary students, Bible school graduates, or Christians in the pew, we do well to heed what Charles Spurgeon once said about election and the doctrines of sovereign grace: "Brethren," he said, "do not try to make the Gospel of God's grace tasteful to carnal minds. Hide not the offense of the cross, lest you make it of none effect. The angles and corners of the Gospel are its strength; to pare them off is to deprive it of power. Toning down is not the increase of strength, but the death of it."

"This is a hard saying."

Election is so important that God devoted one whole chapter of his Word to it. That cannot be said of any other doctrine. It was so important to Christ, who is the pattern for all ministers, that he fully explained it three times. He spoke in the synagogue in his hometown of Nazareth. There he told his friends and neighbors that it was God's prerogative to do as he desired—even to choosing Gentiles over Jews. They were so angry at him that they led him out of the city and tried to throw him off a cliff (Luke 4:24–30). They were *rebels* who refused to believe the doctrine of election.

Jesus also spoke on election in his sermon about himself as the Bread of Life. When he spoke about (spiritually) eating his flesh and drinking his blood, his disciples said, "This is an hard saying; who can hear it?" When Jesus said, "No man can come unto me, except it were given him of my Father," many of his disciples went back, and walked no more with him (John 6:37–66). Those turncoat disciples were also rebels because they refused to accept the biblical doctrine of election.

In his Good Shepherd discourse, Jesus said there were *other* sheep not of the Jewish fold who would come and that only his sheep heard his voice and followed him. The Jews were so incensed they took up stones to stone him (John 10:7–31). Refusing to believe their own Scriptures, those Jews were also rebels.

Bible Conference Hostility

In my early ministry I experienced a small taste of the hostility that Christ experienced when speaking on God's sovereignty and election. I was invited to be one of the speakers at the annual, three-day Bible Conference of the Independent Baptist Churches of Ohio. My sermon title was entitled "Home Town Fickleness," based on Luke, Chapter 4, about Jesus' sermon on election in his hometown of Nazareth.

When I started to speak, I felt that the audience of Baptist ministers were with me. As soon as I got on the subject of election, however, what a change! Some scowled; others shook their heads sideways; and some whispered to each other. I could see that most of those in the audience did not believe the biblical doctrine of election.

Strangely, I was not speaking to Moslems, Buddhists, Hindus, or liberals. I was speaking to Baptist ministers who professed to believe in the divine inspiration of the Scriptures. But they must have believed it with this condition: "Please delete the doctrine of election." From that day on they labeled me "a speckled bird" and "a hyper-Calvinist." Believing the false notion that Calvinists are not mission-minded, they were amazed and could not understand why our church gave so much financially to missions.

His Choice Was Absolute

In his work on *Systematic Theology,* Baptist theologian Augustus Strong said, "Election is that eternal act of God by which in his sovereign pleasure, and on account of no foreseen merit in them, he chooses certain out of the number of sinful men to be recipients of the special grace of his Spirit, and so to be made volunteer partakers of Christ's salvation."[1]

When God chose certain ones to partake of his salvation, his choice was absolute. It was a gracious choice that depended upon nothing outside of God himself. He chose them because he chose to choose them, from no merit, no attraction in the creature to be, but simply out of the spontaneous goodness of his own volition. Out of the mass of all mankind, all of whom were equally guilty and deserving of death, he selected some (a number no man can number) to receive eternal life.

Not Conditional, But Unconditional

Justice demanded that all should die, but justice cannot demand that, if some shall be saved, all must be saved. That was for God to decide. It rested with him to choose all, or none, or some to be saved. Those who were not elected were simply left to themselves and to their sins, and to the just consequences of their sins. The Bible makes it clear that sinners are not saved by their good works. Therefore salvation must be by grace alone.

Some argue that "election means God chose some because he foresaw that they would believe." That is *conditional election*, believing the very concept of which is to deny the biblical doctrine of unconditional election. The Bible teaches that no one has the ability to believe because all are spiritually dead in their trespasses and sins. So there were none whom God could foresee would believe.

It is true that God had the ability to foresee the future, but he did not elect sinners because of what he foresaw in them. His reason for electing some and bypassing others was within himself alone.

God's choice was not only unconditional, it was and is unchangeable. His decree to elect was not founded on anything else. It came before divine foreknowledge. God did not decree election because he

---

1. Dr. Augustus H. Strong, *Systematic Theology* 3 (Philadelphia: The Judson Press, 1942), 779.

foreknew, but he foreknew because in his decree of predestination he foreordained all things that come to pass. To teach otherwise is to say that God decides by guesswork. All he decrees is certain and, since election is certain, it must be established, because he established it.

Eternal and Personal

God's choice is also eternal because "God hath from the beginning chosen you" (2 Thessalonians 2:13; Ephesians 1:4). Since God's electing choice was from the beginning and before the foundation of the world, it was an eternal decree that has no end. It began in eternity and it will last to eternity because nothing can survive to eternity but what came from eternity. "Yea, I have loved thee," said God, "with an everlasting love: therefore with lovingkindness have I drawn thee" (Jeremiah 31:3).

God's choice is personal. Some try to get around the doctrine of unconditional election by saying that election was God's choice of nations, not individuals. "God chose the nation of Israel," they say, "not some in Israel." This is a weak argument because Israel and all other nations were made up of individual persons.

God chose Abraham, Moses, David, Daniel, and thousands more. But he certainly did not choose to elect Korah, Abiram, Dathan, and Judas Iscariot to eternal life.

The Bible says, "God hath chosen us in Christ" (Ephesians 1:4). The word "us" means *believers*, whom Jesus called *sheep* when he said, "He calleth his own sheep by name" (John 10:3). The names of the twelve tribes of Israel were written on the breastplate of the nation's high priest when he served in the tabernacle or temple. In a similar manner, the names of Christ's sheep, those whom God elected to be saved, are written on the breastplate of Jesus Christ, the great High Priest, our surety and our substitute.

Sons we are by God's election,
Who on Jesus Christ believe,

By eternal destination,
Sovereign grace we now receive.

Elected to Be Saved *from* Sin

God's choice of some unto salvation is not only absolute, unchangeable, eternal, and personal, but it is unto holiness. God did not elect sinners to be saved *in* their sin, but to be saved *from* their sin. "God hath from the beginning chosen you unto sanctification of the Spirit and the belief of the truth." That man who claims to be one of God's elect and has a lifestyle of habitual sin is a self contradiction.

God chose the unholy, but they do not remain unholy. God chose the ungodly, but they do not remain ungodly. "Belief of the truth" is a mark of one's election and so is the progressive realization of holiness in his life. One who has been elected and called and born again willingly submits his reason to the teaching of the Word of God. He is not one to believe that old adage "Let your conscience be your guide." Instead, it is the biblical guideline, "Thus saith the Lord" that guides him. Obedience to the Word of God, then, is the evidence of his election.

In his biography of George Whitefield, Arnold Dallimore quotes a letter to John Wesley from George Whitefield in which he explained why he believed in election. "Alas, I never read anything Calvin wrote," he said. "My doctrines I had from Christ and his apostles. I was taught them of God."[2]

ELECTION AS A CONTROVERSIAL TOPIC

It Only Seems *to Be a Contradiction*

Why is election often described as controversial? Election itself is not controversial, but those who rebel against it and refuse to believe

---

2. Arnold Dallimore, *George Whitefield: The Life and Times of the Great Evangelist of the Eighteenth Century Revival* 2 (Carlisle, Pennsylvania: Banner of Truth Trust, 1970 & 1979), 574.

it strive to make it controversial. The controversy, however, is all on their side of the debate. Why do so many people rebel against election and have difficulty receiving this important doctrine?

One answer could be that on the surface election seems to contradict the free offer of the Gospel to all sinners. "And whosoever will," wrote John, "let him take the water of life freely" (Revelation 22:17). Jesus commanded his disciples to go into all the world and preach the Gospel to every creature. And God commands all men everywhere to repent of their sins and their ignorance of God. In the light of these facts, how can it be that salvation is not obtained by human choice, but by God's election?

This seeming contradiction is easily resolved by remembering that the Bible also teaches that men are dead in their trespasses and sins (Ephesians 2:1). Those who come to a true saving faith in Christ come by the sovereign grace of God and not by accident. He brings to faith in Christ as a result of his having chosen them before creation.

"I just can't see election," said a woman to an old Southern minister.

"Madam, did you save yourself," asked the minister, "or did the Lord save you?"

"The Lord saved me."

"Well, did he do it accidentally or on purpose?" A little perturbed, the lady said, "It was on purpose, of course."

"That," said the old preacher, "is election."

Man's Objections to Election

Men seldom admit the true reasons for their opposition to the Gospel of free grace and election. "Election," they say, "will encourage men to sin." They also say that election makes God unfair because he does not save everyone. "Election discourages seekers," they argue, "and makes men careless."

These objections are but camouflage to the real objections. People do not like it and their dignity is offended when the Gospel of free grace tells them they have corrupt hearts, enslaved wills, and evil minds. It goes against their wills to hear Jesus say, "No man can come to me except the Father draw him."

Free grace and election also offend human wisdom when people learn that they are shut up to the divine revelation of the Bible, which says this about all men: "But the natural man receiveth not the things of the Spirit of God: for they are foolishness unto him: neither can he know them, because they are spiritually discerned" (1 Corinthians 2:14).

The very idea of free grace and election also punctures the pride of some because the Gospel teaches that they have to rely on nothing but the merits of Christ alone for salvation, regardless of any act of their own. They do not accept the truth that men are saved not by works of righteousness which they have done, but according to God's mercy.

Free grace and election offends the natural desire in the heart toward sin because the Gospel says that none can be saved unless they meet the perfect requirements of a holy God. Because he is holy, God requires and is satisfied with nothing less than perfection, which can be found only in the Lord Jesus Christ. Scoffers object to those divine requirements for they love darkness rather than light, because their deeds are evil. (John 3:19–20).

ELECTION HAS GREAT VALUE

Election or Free Will

The doctrine of unconditional election has great value because it glorifies the Lord Jesus Christ. There is no other doctrine in the Bible that will shut the sinner up to Christ alone for salvation than the doctrine of election. The world has only two religions: One built upon election and the other on free will. If one adopts the religion built on divine election, he will break down, deny himself, and submit to God and his Word. The one who refuses the religion founded upon election is reduced to asserting his free will.

"Oh, the excellency of the doctrine of election and of the saints final perseverance!" said George Whitefield. "I am persuaded, till a man comes to believe and feel these important truths, he cannot come out of himself, but when convinced of these and assured of their application to his own heart, he then walks by faith indeed."[3]

A sinner going to Christ for salvation often thinks he is doing so under his own power. But election denies that idea. Charles Spurgeon felt the same way. "When I was coming to Christ," he said, "I thought I was doing it all myself and though I sought the Lord earnestly, I had no idea the Lord was seeking me. I do not think the young convert is at first aware of this. I can recall the very day and hour when I first learned those truths (election and sovereign grace) to my own soul, when they were as John Bunyan says, burnt into my heart as with a hot iron. I can recollect how I felt that I had grown on a sudden from a babe to a man, that I had made progress in scriptural knowledge, through having found, once for all, that real clue to the truth of God."

Some Insult the Lord by Not Preaching Election

For one to deny election is to presume that he is wiser than the Lord Jesus Christ. He taught election to his little congregation of disciples, to the crowds at large, to the enemies of the church, and to those who were bent on putting him to death. Any preacher who omits the doctrine of unconditional election in his preaching insults the Lord Jesus Christ and downgrades his ministry.

Besides glorifying Christ, election humbles man. The Lord knows that men and women, because of their sinful nature, are proud and need to be humbled. The way modern evangelists preach Christ today one would think that he was sitting helplessly, waiting for sinners to permit him to save them. Some present Christ as though he were sitting at the right hand of the Father in heaven bewailing the state and condition of earthlings and wondering what he might do to help them.

---

3. Ibid, p. 407.

Not so! Jesus Christ is Lord and by his Spirit he is calling his elect to faith in him at the time appointed for their new birth and conversion. We who are believers can rejoice that we will never hear him say, "Depart from me, I never knew you" (Matthew 7:23).

The Only Way to Happiness

Nothing is more needed by this generation than to know that God owes nothing to sinners but naked justice. As servants of Christ, we need to tell sinners that their hearts are undone in sin, that they are dead to any true sense of the spiritual glory of Christ, and that true, redeeming faith is a gift from God and a work of free grace within their hearts.

Sinners can find happiness only by casting themselves down before the throne of Christ, rejoicing in the truth that God is merciful. To depend upon free will makes a man self-conscious, self-righteous, and proud—like the Pharisees in the time of Jesus' earthly ministry.

George Whitefield was concerned about this need in man. In writing to John Wesley, he urged that they both seek the truth that "shall most debase man and exalt the Lord Jesus. Nothing but the doctrines of the Reformation can do this. All others leave free will in man and make him, in part, at least, a Saviour to himself. I know Christ is all in all. Man is nothing: he hath a free will to go to hell, but none to go to heaven, till God worketh in him to will and to do of his good pleasure."[4]

Calvinism *Versus* Arminianism

The doctrine of election has another value—it is ennobling. Election was taught by John Calvin, and the history of Christianity shows that Calvinism produced more martyrs than Arminianism, which exalted man's free will in salvation. Not many men were willing to die for a free will doctrine. When true revivals came in times past, it was obvious that the preachers who led them proclaimed the doc-

---

4. Ibid, p. 407.

trine of sovereign grace that included the doctrine of unconditional election.

The prime motivation behind the sweeping changes in Europe in the Seventeenth Century and the subsequent colonization of America was mainly the sovereign grace doctrinal preaching, writing, and theology of Martin Luther, John Calvin, Ulrich Zwingli, John Knox, and others.

Later, it was the same Puritan doctrine of election preached by Jonathan Edwards, George Whitefield, and David Brainerd that God used in the Great Awakening revival in the American colonies. It was also the missionary and evangelistic efforts of George Whitefield that transformed the morals and cultures of both England and America.

The Big Thrill of My Life

Man does not need dialogue but confrontation, a moment of truth that shows him that he can be entirely free only when the good Lord sets him free. If preachers refuse to preach election, ecclesiasticism will crowd out the truth and religious ordinances, church forms, ministerial dress, and other religious paraphernalia will take the place of God's eternal Word.

Though I was an athlete in high school and college and a big game hunter after graduation, the greatest thrill in my life was neither an athletic encounter nor a hunting expedition. One of the greatest thrills of my life was to attend a Promise Keepers Rally in the Three Rivers Stadium in Pittsburgh, Pennsylvania. I was sitting in the first row of the second deck looking down on a crowd of twenty-six to forty thousand in the infield and stands.

That huge audience was then asked to stand and sing John Newton's famous hymn, "Amazing Grace." Tears rolled down my face, not just because of those words, "that saved a wretch like me," but with me were my four sons, a son-in-law, and a grandson—all of whom professed faith in the electing love, grace, mercy, and goodness of our Lord Jesus Christ. What thanksgiving, praise, happiness, and gratitude overwhelmed me in that momentous moment before God!

CHAPTER SIX

New but Everlasting

Many Christians haven't a clue as to what the Bible has to say about the subject of covenants. This has come about because many preachers never preach on the subject and most Christians never take the time to study what the Bible actually says about covenants. Yet the Scripture's frequent use of the word "covenant" indicates that to understand the Bible it is imperative to know something about the Lord's covenants.

The Covenantal Concept

Covenants, according to the *Webster's Dictionary,* are "the promises made by God to man as recorded in the Bible." While by no means complete, this isn't a bad definition because the Bible reveals that covenants are unconditional or unilateral contracts by which God agrees with himself that he is going to do something without any assistance from man.

Covenants are an unusual topic because modern Christians are not well-informed on the subject, whereas believers of the past—especially those of the Protestant Reformed tradition—held vigorously to the biblical concept that salvation began with a covenant of grace originated by God before creation. "Salvation," they said, "was the work of the Triune God who, before the foundation of the world, ordained the creation of man, permitted his fall into sin, and ordained his redemption through the shed Blood of Jesus Christ." They also believed that their covenantal concept clearly taught that man could not be saved by his own merit or works, but gave all the glory to God and his grace.

The Historical Baptist Position

Historically, this has been the doctrinal position of most Bible-believing churches. For example, in spite of the many Arminian Baptist churches in America and throughout the world today, who preach a man-centered Gospel, the history of Baptists shows that their belief was the covenant of grace. Many Seventeenth century English Baptists adopted the London Confession and brought it to America, changing it to *The Philadelphia Confession.* Chapter VII, Sections 2 and 3 of that confession read as follows:

> Moreover, man having brought himself under the curse of the law by his fall, it pleased the Lord to make a covenant of grace, wherein he freely offereth unto sinners life and salvation by Jesus Christ, requiring of them faith in him, that they may be saved; and promising to give unto all those who are ordained unto eternal life, his Holy Spirit, to make them willing and able to believe. This covenant is revealed in the Gospel . . . and it is founded in that eternal covenant transaction that was between the Father and the Son about the redemption of the elect.

What a tragedy that many Baptists and a majority of those in the Reformed tradition have forgotten this doctrinal heritage! Few among today's Baptists in America even know about *The Philadelphia Confession* and what it contains. The same is true about Presbyterians, most of whom are not familiar with *The Westminster Confession of Faith.*

For this reason, the Gospel has lost its effectiveness. Mixed with human works, there is more emphasis on organization, invitations, and man's activity than on the grace of God in Jesus Christ.

False Views of the Covenants

The Liberal Attack

There is not only a neglect of the covenant of grace by those who should know better, but some are actually making a determined attack on the teaching of the Bible that there is but one way of salvation. How does this play out?

That arch foe of Christianity called modernism or liberalism is responsible for making the first and deadliest attack on the covenant of grace. This modern system of false theology denies the idea that God supernaturally revealed a plan of salvation by grace. It also denies that man has fallen from grace, and his need to be restored to grace.

Those who believe in liberal theology hate the teaching that "Christ died for our sins" and thereby attempt to destroy the basis upon which we receive the blessings of the covenant of grace. They do not believe that the Bible is a history of God's revelation of himself. On the contrary, they believe that it is simply one account of man's variety of religious experiences.

Believing in evolution, they have no problem accepting the idea that the Bible presents the evolution of religion. For example: Harry Emerson Fosdick, a leading liberal of the Twentieth century once preached on "Progressive Christianity." In that sermon he said this:

> To take a trip through the Bible now is to move from the presence of primitive religion to the noblest expression of the religious spirit in the life of man. To see men's thoughts of God grow from the time they thought of him as a man upon a mountain until they thought of him as the Father of all Creation.

Salvation Has Always Been by Grace

Dispensationalists, who are classified as friends of the Christian faith, also attack the covenant of grace by saying that a person is saved *today* by grace. I emphasize the word *today* because they do not believe that God has always saved by grace and that there is a covenant of grace from eternity to eternity.

Dr. Lewis Sperry Chafer, former president of the Dallas Theological Seminary, proved the existence of this error when he wrote, "There are two widely different, standardized divine provisions, whereby man who is utterly fallen may come into the favor of God. . . . To such a degree as the soteriology of Judaism and the soteriology of Christianity differ, to the same degree do their eschatologies differ."

The first edition of the *Scofield Reference Bible* contains further proof of dispensational attack on the covenant of grace. The author, C. I. Scofield, whose Bible influenced millions to embrace many false ideas especially in the areas of interpretation and prophesy, wrote: "The point of testing is no longer legal obedience as the condition of salvation, but acceptance or rejection of Christ, with good works as a fruit of salvation" (p. 1115).

He also said, "Righteousness here (1 John 3:7) and in the passages having marginal reference to this, means righteous life, which is the result of salvation through Christ. The righteous man under law became righteous by doing righteously; under grace he does righteously because he has been made righteous" (p. 1323).

These footnotes in the *Scofield Reference Bible* were considered to be so erroneous that they were removed from later editions. Both footnotes were heresy. They say that men were saved one way *before* Christ came and another way after he came. In other words, they say there is no eternal covenant of grace. There is an eternal covenant of grace, however, because the Bible declares this fact in one of the greatest benedictions in Scripture. Summing up all that has been said about covenants, it says this:

Now the God of peace, that brought again from the dead our Lord Jesus, that great shepherd of the sheep, through the blood of the

Everlasting Covenant, make you perfect in every good work to do his will, working in you that which is well-pleasing in his sight, through Jesus Christ; to whom be glory for ever and ever. Amen. (Hebrews 13:20–21)

Answers to Questions about the Covenants

Questioning the Number of Covenants

Whenever the subject of biblical covenants comes up, questions arise in our minds that need answering if we are going to understand their meaning and purpose. Those questions have to do with their number, how they are classified, their relationship to one another, and the question, "Is the Everlasting Covenant the same as the New Covenant?"

As to the number of covenants in the Bible, people have different answers. The *Scofield Reference Bible* and most dispensationalists say that there are *eight* covenants in the Bible. They call them: the Edenic, Adamic, Noahic, Abrahamic, Mosaic, Palestinian, Davidic, and the New Covenant.

But others disagree. For example, E. W. Johnson, a scholarly Baptist pastor of Pine Bluff, Arkansas, believes that basically there are only three covenants in the Bible: The covenant God made with Noah (Genesis 6:18; 9:9), the Gospel covenant, and the covenant men make with God in response to the Gospel. He explains his view by saying that the Noahic covenant is the same covenant that God continues to show in progressive revelation to Abraham, Israel, or Moses at Mount Sinai, to David, to Jeremiah and finally the covenant spread before believers at the Lord's Supper.

Most of the Puritans and Charles Haddon Spurgeon said there were only *two* covenants and called them "the covenant of works" and "the covenant of grace."

Covenant of Works?

In my research for this chapter I came upon a little book entitled *The Lord's Supper* by Ernest Kevan, a graduate of London University. After he had served as a Baptist pastor for twenty-two years he was called, in 1946, to be principal of London Bible College. Before his death in 1965, Kevan challenged the view of the Puritans by writing, "I do not think there is any scriptural evidence for what has been theologically called a covenant of works." Kevan was right with regard to the phrase used by the Puritans because the Bible contains no such phrase as the covenant of works.

Even Charles Hodge, one of the greatest theologians of the Nineteenth Century and a teacher to whom the church is greatly indebted, said that "a covenant of works can only be inferred." The Puritans, who had much to say about the covenant of works, all admitted that one could not find the covenant of works in the Bible, but it was a justly inferential concept. Still, assumptions based on inferences are not always correct.

Old and New Covenants

The Scriptures contain a record of *two* covenants: the first or Old Covenant; and the New Covenant. The first covenant, given as it was to Abraham and through him to the Lord's people, was ratified in the time of Moses (Exodus 24:3–8). "And Moses took the blood [of a sacrificed animal] and sprinkled it on the people of Israel and said, 'Behold the blood of the covenant, which the Lord hath made with you concerning all these words'" (Exodus 24:8). That was the authorization of the first covenant.

Arthur W. Pink, in his excellent book *The Divine Covenants,* has a chapter for each of the following covenants: the Everlasting, Adamic, Noahic, Abrahamic, Sinaitic, Davidic, and the Messianic (the name he gives to the New Covenant).

Servants to the New Covenant

From my studies on this subject, I believe that the Bible reveals that the Noahic, Abrahamic, Mosaic, and Davidic covenants are all part of the Old Covenant. It was Jeremiah the prophet who announced the coming of a New Covenant—a promise that was fulfilled centuries later in the person and ministry and Gospel of the Lord Jesus Christ. I believe that Ernest Kevan was scriptural when he said there were two covenants, the Old and the New or the first and the second.

I believe that the Noahic, Abrahamic, Mosaic, and Davidic covenants were but servants to the New Covenant. The New Covenant or, as the writer to the Hebrews called it, the Everlasting Covenant, was before them all, and outlasts them all. It is new only in human experience, but it was conceived and established in the eternal counsels, embracing the vast sweep of God's divine purposes.

The Basis or Foundation of the New or Everlasting Covenant

"They shall be my people."

So far we have learned that Moses ratified the first or Old Covenant with the sprinkling of sacrificial blood. Hundreds of years later, the prophet Jeremiah announced the New Covenant with these words:

> Behold, the days come, saith the LORD, that I will make a New Covenant with the house of Israel, and with the house of Judah: Not according to the covenant that I made with their fathers in the day that I took them by the hand to bring them out of the land of Egypt; which my covenant they brake, although I was an husband unto them, saith the LORD: But this shall be the covenant that I will make with the house of Israel; After those days, saith the LORD, I will put my law in their inward parts, and write it in their hearts; and will be their God, and they shall be my people. And they shall teach no more every man his neighbor, and every man his brother, saying, Know the LORD: for they shall all know me, from the least of them unto the greatest of them, saith the LORD: for I will forgive their iniquity, and I will remember their sin no more. (Jeremiah 31:31–34)

The Feast of the New Covenant

Notice that there is something missing here. In the inauguration of the first covenant, the terms of the covenant were first enunciated and then ratified by the sprinkling of shed blood. There is an incompleteness in Jeremiah's account of the New Covenant. The terms are declared, but it is like a legal document which has not been signed and witnessed. There is no ratifying *blood*.

The people of the Lord had to wait six centuries for that ratification. Then, surrounded by his twelve closest associates in an upper room in Jerusalem at the Feast of the Passover, the Lord Jesus foretold his own death. As he handed the cup of remembrance to his disciples, he said, "This is my blood of the New Covenant which is shed for many for the remission of sins." Notice how much is included in the words, "which is shed for many for the remission of sins."

Those were the terms and promises of the New Covenant first announced by Jeremiah. And after the centuries had rolled off into the past, the Lord said, in effect, "This is the New Covenant which I am about to ratify with my own Blood." For this reason, the Lord's Supper is the feast of the New Covenant and is the basis or visible sign of this Covenant, just as that of the Old Covenant was the shedding of animals' blood. The New Covenant is superior in every way to the Old Covenant. So is its ratification. The Blood of the New Covenant was not the blood of animals, but none other than the Blood of the spotless, eternal Son of God!

Primitive tribes still follow the ancient custom of sealing their covenants with blood. Even in civilized countries, men have used blood to express the irrevocableness of their undertaking. In the Greyfriars Churchyard in Edinburgh on the twenty-eighth day of February, 1638, the brave men of Scotland swore their allegiance to church and king in the National Covenant of Scotland. Some of the men "did draw their own blood and used it instead of ink." By signing his name to the covenant in his own blood, each man was saying, "My life for it."

Symbol and Sacrifice

The precious Blood of Christ at once obtained the redemption sought, and sealed the new or Everlasting Covenant. The whole mystery of the Incarnation of the Son of God is wrapped up in the New Covenant. Since it required the shedding of blood, he must needs have blood to shed. Therefore the Bible says, "For verily he took not on him the nature of angels; but he took on him the seed of Abraham." *Why?* That he might have the eternal covenant made over to him, "a great multitude, which no man could number, of all nations, and kindreds, and people and tongues" (Hebrews 2:16). A vast sea of redeemed and, because of him, victorious sinners!

When we partake of the Lord's Supper, the wine is not representative merely of the blood of him who loved us; it is the symbol of the blood of a covenant sacrifice. That sacrifice in a covenant relationship was an act in which God committed himself in the most solemn way possible. Many Evangelical churches celebrate this truth in the grand old hymn, "The Solid Rock." Here is the third verse of that hymn:

> His oath, his covenant, and his blood,
> Support me in the whelming flood;
> When all around my soul gives way,
> He then is all my hope and stay.

Christ Confirmed the Covenant

In the blood of Christ we have the ground of our assurance, a sure covenant, and a ratified pledge to plead. This is what the Lord Jesus meant when he held out the cup and said, "This is the New Covenant *in my blood*" (emphasis mine). That little word "in" was translated from a Greek word which means "resting upon."

In those words the Son of God did not present himself as one who inaugurated the New Covenant, but rather as the means of its confirmation. The infinite, eternal, and holy, triune God is the author of the Everlasting Covenant and the one who inaugurated it.

Discarding Hymns about the Blood

The blood of Christ is very important in God's plan to redeem a people for himself. It is correct to speak of the death of Christ because by his death he bore our guilt away; but we must be careful how we use that expression. I say this because the "death of Christ" and the "blood of Christ," strictly speaking, are not synonymous terms.

The blood of Christ points to something more than the death of Christ. Gathered up into the blood of Christ is all the connotation of sacrifice, of covenant, and of guarantee. Therefore, "the blood of Christ" is one of the most sacred and significant phrases in the Bible.

Some people object to the use of the word *blood* in our religious vocabulary because it offends their sensibilities. Some denominations and their publishing houses have even deleted hymns about the blood of Christ from their hymn books. Such action reveals an ignorance of the very essence of salvation truth in both the Old and New Testaments. Hebrews 9:11–22 makes this truth so plain that Christians *should* be able to understand it.

Verse 22 says that "almost all things are by the law purged with blood; and without shedding of blood is no remission." In the next chapter we read, "Now where the remission of these [sins] is, there is no more offering for sin. Having therefore, brethren, boldness to enter into the holiest [holy of holies] by the blood of Jesus . . ." (Hebrews 10:18–19). Clearly, God left no doubt concerning the importance of covenantal blood.

He Refused the Blood and Died

How foolish is that person who rejects the blood of Christ! During World War II a wounded Nazi soldier was taken prisoner on one of the battlefields of France. Bleeding profusely but still conscious, he was rushed to a field hospital behind the lines. As a doctor was about to give him a blood transfusion, the Nazi soldier demanded to know the source of the blood.

"It is from an English blood bank," he was told. When he heard that, he refused the blood and died in a few hours. What a picture this is of the thousands of sinners today who refuse to receive the blood of Christ—their only hope of eternal salvation!

The Superiority of the New and Everlasting Covenant

Not Trial and Error

In a study of the covenants we cannot afford to miss this important information in God's Word: "For if that first covenant had been faultless, then should no place be sought for the second. . . . In that he saith, A new covenant, he hath made the first old. Now that which decayeth and waxeth old is ready to vanish away" (Hebrews 8:7,13).

Hebrews, Chapter 8 frankly admits the faultiness of the first or earlier covenant. This does not mean that God was operating on the trial and error principle, however. He was not *testing* the Levitical covenant with a view to discovering the better or New Covenant out of the defects revealed by the experiment. Rather, he had a different plan.

An Unbearable Burden

The first covenant was not faulty for its given purpose, but it was inadequate to fulfill God's ultimate aims. Indeed, the fault of the Old Covenant was necessary for God's immediate intention. God designed the Old Covenant to reveal the insufficiency of man, which was proved when they found the terms of the Old Covenant a burden too heavy to bear.

This point was brought up at the first church council in Jerusalem. Some of those in attendance said that the early Gentile converts should be circumcised and should obey the Old Covenant law. In response, Peter the apostle said this: "Now therefore why tempt ye God, to put a yoke upon the neck of the disciples, which neither our fathers nor we were able to bear" (Acts 15:10).

When Moses read the book of the covenant in the audience of the people of Israel they embraced it without hesitation, not stopping to question whether they had the ability to meet its demands. "All that the Lord hath said," they declared, "will we do, and be obedient" (Exodus 24:7).

It remained for all their history to discover their instability under that Covenant of Obedience, and to see that there was nothing in the covenant itself to mend a faulty people. God planned the New Covenant before the foundation of the world and it was in his heart *before* he made the older one with the nation of Israel. All during the days of failure, when the Old Covenant of law showed itself to be inadequate, and the covenant people displayed their inability to keep its holy terms, God progressively revealed the *better* covenant that was to come.

Applicable to More than Jews

There came a time when the people's breach of the covenant had become complete, and the Lord's fierce and just anger was about to break upon the unfaithful nation. At that time in history the Lord gave the terms of the New Covenant to the prophet Jeremiah: "Behold the days come," said the Lord, "that I will make a New Covenant with the house of Israel, and with the house of Judah" (Jeremiah 31:31).

The New Covenant, however, was applicable to more than the Jewish nation. Writing by divine inspiration, the apostle said it was none other than the Eternal Covenant that was extended to all the world. It was according to this covenant that the Son of God accomplished redemption for the elect of all nations.

Here is one way by which the New Covenant is clearly superior to the old. It is wider in its embrace and not confined to one nation. It reaches out in equal grace to all who are in the Everlasting Covenant.

Grace Met All the Law's Demands

The faultiness of the Old Covenant was corrected in the New. The intolerable burden the people could not bear because of their inherent inability was removed. What the law demanded, grace undertook to meet. The terminology changed from the Old Covenant's "Thou shalt" to the New Covenant's "I will." The inability of man to save himself having now been fully demonstrated, God was ready to make full proof of his grace.

"For what the law could not do, in that it was weak through the flesh," wrote Paul the Apostle, "God sending his own Son in the likeness of sinful flesh, and for sin, condemned sin in the flesh: that the righteousness of the law might be fulfilled in us, who walk not after the flesh, but after the Spirit" (Romans 8:3–4).

Though the terms of the New Covenant show that it is a covenant of grace, they also show that it does not repudiate (or deny) the law. For example, in announcing the New Covenant God said, "I will put my laws into their minds, and write them in their hearts" (Hebrews 8:10). This means that men and women receive the law by an inward disposition instead of by an outward *imposition*.

Concerning this fact, Andrew Murray suggested an interesting analogy: "Why does an acorn so spontaneously grow up into an oak? Because the law of the oak is written in the heart of the acorn. There is nothing forced, nothing legalistic, about that. Yet it is law."

As one of the Puritans is quoted to have said, "All is law, yet all is grace."

Not by Compulsion, *But by* Impulsion

Jesus said the whole law is comprehended in these two commandments: "Thou shalt love the Lord thy God with all thy heart, and with all thy soul, and with all thy mind, and with all thy strength: this is the first commandment. And the second is like it, namely this: Thou shall love thy neighbor as thyself" (Mark 12:30–31).

Where there is true love for God and man there is no need for the compulsion of law. One does not lie to, steal from, or exercise violence against a person he loves. Paul taught the same thing when he began his description of the fruit of the Spirit with love. We obey, therefore, not by compulsion of law but by impulsion of the love of God which has been "shed abroad in our hearts by the Holy Ghost" (Romans 5:5).

The inscribing of God's law upon our hearts marks an immutable union between God and the believer. "And I will be a God to them," says the Lord, "and they shall be to me a people" (Hebrews 8:10).

He Stole Spurgeon's Cane

Charles Spurgeon once received from John B. Gough an ebony walking stick with a gold head studded with California quartz. One night a thief sneaked into Spurgeon's house and stole his expensive walking stick.

When he got home, the thief hammered off the gold head and tried to sell it to a pawnbroker. In examining it, the pawnbroker discovered the name, S-P-U-R-G-E-O-N, printed on it. When he asked the thief to wait a minute, the man took off. Though marred by the hammering, the inscription indicated ownership, and the pawnbroker returned the gold head to Spurgeon.

Our adversary the devil may do all in his power to separate us from God, but God's law inscribed in our hearts settles the relationship between him and us. And that relationship will stand forever. Since we have the witness of the Holy Spirit within us, we do not have to pray as David did when he said, "Cast me not away from thy presence; and take not thy Holy Spirit from me" (Psalm 51:11).

A Divine Arrangement

Christians usually think of a covenant in the Bible as an agreement that is made between God and man, yet that is but a consequent aspect of it. The destiny of man was indeed a subject of concern in the New Covenant, but the covenant was essentially a divine arrangement in which the Father promised to undertake the exaltation of his beloved Son, the Lord Jesus Christ. Here is how David described the substance of that promise in Psalm 2:7–8:

I will declare the decree: The Lord hath said unto me, "Thou art my Son; This day have I begotten thee. Ask of me and I shall give thee the heathen for thine inheritance, and the uttermost parts of the earth for thy possession."

The Lord Jesus calls those who have been saved from their sins his *children* whom his Father gave to him. Quoting Isaiah 8:18, he said, "Behold, I and the children which God hath given me" (Hebrews 2:13). And again, "All that the Father giveth me shall come to me; and him that cometh to me I will in no wise cast out" (John 6:37).

Given in covenant by the Father to the Son, the children were sinners before their conversion. They were children of wrath, enemies, aliens, slaves to sin, guilty, vile, and helpless. Before Christ could claim them for his own peculiar treasure, however, he had to give himself in sacrifice for their sins. This he did, and the promise of children to Christ involves their glorious redemption by his own shed blood.

The New Covenant Is Superior

The New Covenant of grace provides and secures such blessings for the children as will make them fit to be the Lord's inheritance. The blessings of the elect can no more fail than God's covenant with his Son can be broken. Thus the New Covenant gathers us into its mighty sweep; it becomes ours, as if God had entered into it directly and primarily with us.

There is also a superiority to the new or everlasting covenant because the Bible says that when we come unto the city of the living God and the heavenly Jerusalem we come "to Jesus the mediator of the New Covenant, and to the blood of sprinkling, that speaketh better things than that of Abel" (Hebrews 12:24). The importance of the covenant and the sealing blood of Jesus Christ can also be seen in these lines:

In this the covenant is sealed,
And heaven's eternal grace revealed;
Great God of wonders, all thy ways,
Are matchless, godlike, and divine,
But the fair glories of thy grace,
More godlike and unrivaled shine.
Who is a pardoning God like thee,
Or who has grace so rich and free?

CHAPTER SEVEN

The Greatest Embrace in History

The most touching scenes of the military action *Desert Storm* did not take place in the Middle East, but on the docks and air bases of America. Scenes of hundreds of tear-filled embraces were televised as soldiers, sailors, and airmen said goodbye to loved ones before they departed to take part in the Gulf War. A few months later, those scenes were reenacted and again televised for all to see. Only this time the tears were tears of joy as thousands of returning men and women of the military were welcomed in loving embrace.

I happened to be watching television the day Commanding General "Stormin' Norman" Schwarzkopf landed in America. What a scene it was to see him embrace his wife and daughters with a tremendous hug accompanied by kisses! It reminded me of wise King Solomon's words: "There is a time to embrace and a time to refrain from embracing" (Ecclesiastes 3:5). After a victorious military campaign with so few casualties, that surely *was* a time to embrace.

Biblical Embraces

The word "embrace" or "embracing" appears only fourteen times in the English Bible—eleven times in the Old Testament and three times in the New. Genesis uses the word three times concerning Jacob. The story says that his Uncle Laban embraced and kissed him; his brother Esau embraced and kissed him after years of separation; and, prior to his death, Jacob embraced the sons of Joseph.

In the New Testament, Paul embraced a young man named Eutychus who had fallen from a third loft where Paul was preaching. As the Christians gathered around the prostrate form, they were certain that the lad was dead. Paul, however, fell on him, and embracing him said, "Trouble not yourselves for his life is in him" (Acts 20:10).

The last use of embrace is in Hebrews 11:13. Speaking of the heroes of the faith, it says, "These all died in faith, not having received the promises, but having seen them afar off, and were persuaded of them and embraced them, and confessed that they were strangers and pilgrims on the earth" (Hebrews 11:13).

Three Definite Subjects

Reading a passage like this one, each of us should ask himself, "Have I embraced the promises of God? Have I embraced the greatest promise in the Bible—God's promise of a Messiah, Jesus Christ, the Lord and Saviour of all who believe in him?" The greatest embrace of all history also had to do with Jesus Christ and God's plan to redeem a people for himself. I have included it as an *unusual topic* because not many Christians have even thought about it. The greatest embrace is found in the text we are going to look at in this chapter: Psalm 85:10:

Mercy and truth are met together;
Righteousness and peace have kissed each other.

This passage suggests three definite subjects. If you would like to become more familiar with the divine plan of redemption, take the time to learn, believe, and apply the practical aspects of these subjects to your own Christian life. The subjects are: 1) Intimate Cooperation in the Purpose of God; 2) The Only Perfect Plan of Salvation; and 3) God's Guarantee of a Wonderful Future.

INTIMATE COOPERATION IN THE PURPOSE OF GOD

Four Attributes of God

The four key words of Psalm 85:10 are names or attributes of God: mercy, truth, righteousness and peace. *Mercy,* for example, was mentioned by Moses when he said that God was merciful.

The psalmist David also wrote that God's tender mercy is over all his works. And in the New Testament Paul declared that God is rich in mercy and is the "Father of Mercies." *Truth is* also a quality and name of God. Moses and Isaiah described him as the God of truth. And Jesus Christ proved he was God when he said, "I am the truth" (John 14:6).

Peace, a word that can be found scores of times in the Bible, also belongs to God. Writing to believers in Thessalonica, Paul said, "The very God of peace sanctify you." And to the church at Ephesus, he wrote that they had been "made nigh by the blood of Christ, for he is our peace." He also told the Corinthians that "God is not the author of confusion, but of peace."

Righteousness, one of the most important words in the Bible, is a name of God. The Hebrew, *Jehovah Tsidkenu* means "The Lord our Righteousness" (Jeremiah 23:6; 33:16). At the fall of Adam, Mercy was ever-inclined to save man and peace could not be man's enemy. Truth, however, exacted the performance of God's threat, "The soul that sinneth, it shall die" (Ezekiel 18:4).

Since God is true in all his ways and righteous in all his works, his righteousness could not but give to everyone his just due. In the person of Jesus Christ, as the Saviour of elect sinners, truth and mercy came together and righteousness and peace kissed each other.

There is no other religion on earth except true, Bible-based Christianity that can satisfy the demands of these claimants and restore a union between them. Only the religion of Christ and his apostles can show how God's Word can be true, his work just, and how the sinner, notwithstanding, can find mercy and obtain peace.

Trouble Believing the Trinity

Though they enjoy the blessings of God's mercy and peace, few Christians really understand the doctrine of the trinity—that the Godhead is three persons in one: God the Father, God the Son, and God the Holy Spirit. Many say they believe in a triune God, but their faith, prayers, and actions do not reflect the truth that the three persons of the Godhead are coequal, coeternal, and cooperative in creation, providence, and redemption.

Once as a pastor in New York State I had an appointment with a prosperous Christian businessman. He was a conservative believer and a member of the Methodist Church. During our theological discussion, he said he was upset because his denomination was getting away from the Bible and from sound doctrine. Then he made a statement that I have never heard before nor since.

"I think too much emphasis is placed upon Jesus Christ and not enough emphasis upon the Father," he said. I reminded him that Jesus said, "I and the Father are one" (John 10:30); and that "He that hath seen me hath seen the Father" (John 14:9). I noted also that in praying to God the Father about his disciples, Jesus had also said, "And the glory which thou gavest me I have given them: that they may be one, even as we are one" (John 17:22).

Although that fine Christian businessman believed the great doctrines of the Christian faith, he was misinformed about the doctrine of the trinity. He was wrong to say that more emphasis should be given to God the Father than to God the Son, for the three persons of the Godhead are equal in all qualities of being such as love, grace, mercy, power, wisdom, righteousness, justice, holiness, and purpose. We must always think of the infinite God in that coequal way.

Trinity and the Word "Must"

John used the word "must" eight times in his Gospel. All of these instances are important, but not as important as the three times he used *must* with regard to the trinity. First, he quoted Jesus as saying, "Ye must be born again" (John 3:7). This surely has to do with the Holy Spirit and his sovereign and independent work of regeneration.

Second, he also quoted Christ as saying, "The Son of man must be lifted up: that whosoever believeth in him should not perish, but have eternal life" (John 3:14–15). This refers to God the Son, who must needs give his lifeblood in order to make atonement for sinners.

And third, he quoted Christ as saying, "God is a Spirit: and they that worship him must worship him in spirit and in truth" (John 4:24). This has reference to God the Father as the object of sincere worship. The order here cannot be changed. Only those who have been regenerated by God the Holy Spirit, and justified by the atonement of God the Son, can worship God the Father. The Bible says that "the sacrifice [or worship] of the wicked is an abomination to the Lord" (Proverbs 15:8).

Notice how imperative Jesus was in his use of the word "must" and how he declared that there was no alternative to how we are to worship God. He gave no choice in the matter. His "must" was final!

Cooperation in the Godhead

There is a finality, as well, in the intimate cooperation of the members of the Godhead. "The Son can do nothing of himself," said Jesus, "but what he seeth the Father do: for what things soever he doeth, these also doeth the Son likewise" (John 5:19).

In one of his great discourses Jesus pointed to the intimate co-operation of the Godhead when he said that it was the Holy Spirit who quickens or *makes alive,* for the flesh profits nothing (John 6:63). Shortly after he had raised Lazarus from the grave, Jesus again revealed the intimate cooperation of the Godhead when he said, "For

I have not spoken of myself; but the Father who sent me, he gave me a commandment, what I should say, and what I should speak" (John 12:49).

Jesus also exhibited trinitarian cooperation when he said that God the Father would send God the Holy Spirit in the name of God the Son (John 14:26). The intimacy and cooperation enjoyed by the three persons of the Godhead can be seen in these words of Jesus in John 16:13–15:

> Howbeit when he, the Spirit of truth, is come, he will guide you into all truth: for he shall not speak of himself; but whatsoever he shall hear, that shall he speak: and he will shew you things to come. He shall glorify me: for he shall receive of mine, and shall shew it unto you. All things that the Father hath are mine: therefore said I, that he shall take of mine, and shall shew it unto you.

A Better Understanding

As we read these words of our blessed Saviour we can more clearly understand the events that took place when he was baptized by John the Baptist. "And Jesus, when he was baptized, went up straightway out of the water: and, lo, the heavens were opened unto him, and he saw the Spirit of God descending like a dove, and lighting upon him: And lo a voice from heaven, saying, 'This is my beloved Son, in whom I am well pleased'" (Matthew 3:16–17).

It is no wonder that in the Garden of Gethsemane prior to his death Jesus prayed, "Father, the hour is come; glorify thy Son, that thy Son also may glorify thee" (John 17:1). Neither should we be amazed at what Jesus said after his Resurrection. Appearing in the locked room where the disciples were assembled for fear of the Jews who had instigated Christ's Crucifixion, Jesus breathed on them and said, "Receive ye the Holy Ghost" (John 20:22).

THE ONLY PERFECT PLAN OF SALVATION

Only One Perfect Plan of Salvation

"Mercy and truth," said the Psalmist, "are met together; righteousness and peace have kissed each other" (85:10). What an embrace! What a revelation! These words reveal not only the intimate cooperation of the Godhead, but the truth that there is only one perfect plan of salvation.

Mercy, truth, righteousness, and peace. Mercy and truth on one side; righteousness and peace on the other. Truth requires righteousness and mercy calls for peace. They meet on the way: one going to make inquiry and punishment for sin; the other going to plead for reconciliation. Having met, they adjust their differences and blend. Then, mutual claims in one common interest of peace and righteousness immediately embrace. Thus righteousness is given to truth and peace is given to mercy.

The question arises, "Where did these two meet, and when were they reconciled?" They met in the person of Jesus Christ and they were reconciled when he poured out his life on the Cross of Calvary. "Mercy and truth are met together" in God for the Bible says, "All the paths of the Lord are mercy and truth unto such as keep his covenant and his testimonies" (Psalm 25:10).

Paul the Apostle of Christ emphasized this truth in Romans 15:8–9, where he wrote, "Now I say that Jesus Christ was a minister of the circumcision for the truth of God, to confirm the promises made unto the fathers: And that the Gentiles might glorify God for his mercy." God promised his Son unto the Jews; and in the fullness of time, he gave him to be both a light to the Gentiles and the glory of his people Israel. In this way he showed his mercy more to the Gentiles and his truth unto the Jews. His mercy and truth, therefore, embrace each other in that he makes both people to be one, to wit, *one* flock under one Shepherd.

Righteousness, the One Requirement

To become a member of that one flock and be sure of heaven, the one thing we all require is righteousness. "How can this be true," asks one, "when the Bible teaches that sinners *have* no righteousness?"

That is a good question because the Bible does teach that "there is none righteous, no, not one" (Romans 3:10). It also says, "We are all as an unclean thing, and all our righteousnesses [the very best things we can do] are as filthy rags" (Isaiah 64:6). John showed the impossibility of a sinner without righteousness getting into the one flock and being right with God. "Whosoever doeth not righteousness," he said, "is not of God" (1 John 3:10).

"That being true," says the sinner, "how then can I get right with God and go to heaven when I die?"

The only way of salvation, the only way a sinner can get right with God and be sure of heaven, is to experience a bi-directional imputation. This experience comes to the sinner by the grace of God through faith in Jesus Christ. When a sinner truly believes in Jesus Christ as his Lord and Saviour, God imputes his guilt to Christ and Christ's righteousness or *innocence* to Him. Once that bi-directional imputation takes place, God is in a legal position to justify the sinner or declare him to be righteous in his sight.

If we were to depend on our own righteousness for salvation, we would be lost. That is why it is imperative that we receive what theologians call "an alien righteousness"—a righteousness that is not our own, but which comes from outside of ourselves. That is what the Epistle to the Romans is all about.

The sinner who is declared righteous in God's sight is seen as having Christ's righteousness and he can never be called before the heavenly tribunal and declared guilty for the sins he has committed. "Who can lay anything to the charge of God's elect?" asked Paul. "It is God that justifieth" (Romans 8:33).

The Lord Our Righteousness

Having Christ's righteousness imputed to us gives us an amazingly close relationship to God because righteousness is one of his names. As we learned earlier, this is the meaning of the Hebrew words, *Jehovah Tsidkenu:* "The Lord our righteousness."

This truth had such an impact on the heart of a young preacher in Scotland that he wrote what I think to be one of the best hymns in all Christendom. His name was Robert Murray M'Cheyne, and he was pastor of the Free Church of Dundee, Scotland. "M'Cheyne's memory," said one biographer, "is like ointment poured on a burning wound."

Though M'Cheyne died before he was twenty-nine years old his godly life and his writings have left an influence for good and the Gospel for more than a hundred and fifty years. Reading or singing the words of this his hymn always brings tears to my eyes because M'Cheyne's confession is McNeill's confession. I trust that it is, or that it will also become, your confession. Here is what Robert Murray M'Cheyne wrote on the eighteenth of November, 1834, just nine years before he died:

> I once was a stranger to grace and to God,
> I knew not my danger, and felt not my load;
> Though friends spoke in rapture of Christ on the tree,
> Jehovah Tsidkenu was nothing to me.

> I oft read with pleasure, to soothe or engage,
> Isaiah's wild measure, and John's simple page;
> But e'n when they pictured the blood-stained tree,
> Jehovah Tsidkenu seemed nothing to me.

> Like tears from the daughters of Zion that roll
> I wept when the waters went over my soul;
> Yet thought not that my sins had nailed to the tree
> Jehovah Tsidkenu—'twas nothing to me.

When free grace awoke me, with light from on high
Then legal fears shook me, I trembled to die;
No refuge, no safety, in self could I see,
Jehovah Tsidkenu my Saviour must be.

My terrors all vanished before that sweet Name;
My guilty fears banished, with boldness I came
To drink at the fountain, life-giving and free,
Jehovah Tsidkenu is all things to me.

Jehovah Tsidkenu! My treasure and boast;
Jehovah Tsidkenu! I ne'er can be lost;
In thee I shall conquer, by flood and by field
My cable, my anchor, my breastplate and shield!

The Two Testaments Met in Christ

Righteousness and peace met in Christ, God's Son, the last Adam. Some expositors think that righteousness and peace may also stand for the Old Testament and the New Testament. The Law of the Old Testament exacted justice that required of a malefactor an eye for an eye, a tooth for a tooth, a hand for a hand, and a foot for a foot. The Gospel, however, is full of mercy and peace, saying unto the repentant sinner, "Son, be of good comfort, thy sins are forgiven thee," or, "Daughter, be of good cheer, thy faith hath made thee whole," or "Behold, thou art made whole, sin no more." The two Testaments met in Christ, embraced and kissed each other because the Gospel accomplished redemption by meeting all the penal demands of the law.

In telling the story of the Prodigal Son (Luke 15:11–24), Christ said that the prodigal's father, seeing his lost son in misery a great way off, ran to him, fell on his neck, and kissed him. One cannot but feel that this touching, tender story from the lips of our Saviour is a beautiful illustration of Psalm 85:10: "Mercy and truth are met together; righteousness and peace have kissed each other."

God's Guarantee of a Wonderful Future

Never Allow Yourself to Be Deceived

Psalm 85:10 seals the many promises about the believer's future with God when he will right all the wrongs of history. Though Psalm 85 contains only thirteen verses, the Psalmist used the word "truth" twice, the word "peace" twice, and the word "righteousness" three times. Yet these three subjects seem to be missing in so much of the activity of men and women. Unbelievers who hate the truth think they have them on the scaffold in their attempts to destroy them.

We should never allow ourselves to be deceived because millions of this world's inhabitants think, live, and speak in opposition to God's truth, peace, and righteousness. Here is the infidel Thomas Paine, for example, in the summation of his destructive, anti-Bible work, *The Age of Reason:*

> I have gone through the Bible as a man would go through a wood with an axe on his shoulder, felling trees. Here they lie; and the priests, if they can, may replant them. They may, perhaps, stick them in the ground but they will never make them grow.

Thomas Paine is dead, but God's Word will never die. Jesus said it would endure forever because its divine author is eternal, sovereign, and always right. The annual publication of an estimated fifty million copies of God's Word has proven the falsity of the foolish prophecy of Thomas Paine, the infidel. Having faced the Judge of all the earth, he no doubt now knows just how wrong he was!

God Has Stopped Winking

The Bible teaches that the thoughts, actions, and even the idle words of men will be judged. The certainty of judgment is guaranteed because mercy and truth have met together and righteousness and peace have embraced and kissed each other. Speaking to the philosophers of Athens, Paul pointed to that certain judgment when he said this:

> And the times of this ignorance God winked at; but now commandeth all men everywhere to repent: Because he hath appointed a day, in the which he will judge the world in righteousness by that man whom he hath ordained; whereof he hath given assurance unto all men, in that he hath raised him from the dead. (Acts 17:30–31)

Some find the phrase "And the times of this ignorance God winked at" difficult to understand. Weymouth translated it to read, "Those times of ignorance God viewed with indulgence." The New International Version reads, "In the past God overlooked such ignorance." Commenting on this passage, the notes in the *New Geneva Study Bible* include this statement:

> Truly these times of ignorance God overlooked. That is, God took into consideration the limitations of their knowledge about God, but now Paul has revealed the truth about the living God. With all people they are called on to repent of their sins.[1]

These Will Receive God's Most Severe Punishment

Of all the impenitent sinners at their time of judgment, have you ever wondered on whom God will be the most severe? I think he will reserve his most severe punishment for those who have denied and mocked his truth, who have rejected or manipulated the Gospel doctrine of Christ. These will include false Christs, false teachers, false prophets, false preachers, liberals, modernists, hypocrites, and proud religionists. Speaking of the liberals of his day and commenting on Psalm 85:10, Charles Spurgeon said this:

---

1. *New Geneva Study Bible, New King James Version* (Thomas Nelson Publishers, Nashville, Atlanta, London, Vancouver), 1743.

The inner sense of this text is Jesus Christ, the reconciling word. In Christ, the attributes of God unite in a glad unanimity in the salvation of guilty men. They embrace in an inconceivable manner to relieve our just fears and to enlighten our hopes. It is the custom of modern thinkers to make sport of this representation and the results of our Lord's substitutionary atonement, but had they even been themselves made to feel the weight of sin upon a spiritually awakened conscience, they would cease from their vain ridicule. Their doctrine of atonement has been described as the admission that the Lord Jesus Christ did something or other, which somehow or other was in some way or other connected with man's salvation. This is their substitute for the doctrine of substitution.

Our facts are infinitely superior to their dreams, and yet they sneer. It is but natural that natural men should do so. We cannot expect animals to be moved by the discoveries of science; neither can we hope to see unspiritual men rightly estimate the solution of spiritual problems. They are far above and out of their sight. Meanwhile it remains for those who rejoice in the great reconciliation to continue both to wonder and adore.[2]

He Destroys the Flesh to Save the Spirit

Not only unbelievers but even some believers of this generation act and talk as though God was not on the throne of the universe. They act as though mercy and truth have not met together and that righteousness and peace have not kissed each other. Just as the mercies of wicked men are laced with cruelty, so the judgments of God are filled with mercy. In his wrath he remembers pity; he punishes a little that he might pardon a great deal; and he destroys the flesh to save the spirit (1 Corinthians 5:5).

Looking back on the sufferings of some we can see that they profited by them. For example, it was good for Joseph to be sold

---

2. Charles H. Spurgeon, *Treasury of David* (Grand Rapids, Michigan: Zondervan Publishing House), 453.

into slavery and imprisoned on false charges, for Naaman to suffer from leprosy, for Bartimaeus to suffer blindness, and for David to be hounded by King Saul. Puritan William Bradford thanked the Lord more for his prison terms than for any parlor or pleasure he had otherwise known.

We may not recognize it at the time but all things are for the best unto the faithful. The tribulations and blessings in our lives show that mercy and truth are met together and that righteousness and peace have kissed each other. God's mercy is just and his justice is merciful. When he gave his only Son to a sinful world he showed more abundantly that his mercy and justice embraced and kissed each other.

"Kiss the Son," says David, "lest he be angry, and ye perish from the way, when his wrath is kindled but a little. Blessed are all they that put their trust in him" (Psalm 2:12).

The attributes of God embrace, kiss, and are displayed in our salvation. Mercy in the promise, truth in its fulfillment, righteousness in the manner of its fulfillment, and peace in its results. They all meet in the person of Jesus Christ, which means they meet, embrace, and kiss in the everlasting covenant, at the incarnation of Christ, at the cross on Calvary, at the empty tomb, at the conversion of every sinner, and, finally, at the glorification of the saints in heaven.

Truly *this* was the greatest embrace in history!

CHAPTER EIGHT

The Called

"I wish the Gospel," said Thomas Boston, "was always called by its right name, *glad tidings,* then we should know better what we are about. Now the offer of glad tidings is simply absurd; it is nonsense. Glad tidings are not offered, but rather proclaimed, made known, published. It is the 'Gospel of the grace of God,' the glad tidings of the grace of God, that salvation is all of grace; and this is the Gospel to be preached to every creature. Neither do I hesitate to say that those, however high-sounding their names, who deal indiscriminately in offers and invitations to dead sinners, are false teachers."[1]

I, Too, Have a Wish!

Like Boston, I too have a wish. I wish that those who believe in our Lord Jesus Christ would be labeled by other names or terms than Methodists, Presbyterians, Pentecostals, Lutherans, Baptists, and Episcopalians. This is not to minimize the importance of denomina-

---

1. Thomas Boston was a Scottish evangelical minister of the eighteenth century and a noted authority on the Hebrew Bible. He had a great influence on others because of his faithful and exemplary dedication to his parochial tasks and by the 12 volumes of his popular writings.

tions, because a man's denomination often signifies what he believes. Church membership is important and every person who has been saved through faith in Christ should, wherever possible, become a member of a Bible-believing, local, Christian church.

The word "Christian" is found three times in the New Testament, but the Bible also uses several other terms to identify Christians. Those terms are "brethren," "believers," "children of God," "children of light," "disciples," "the elect," "those of the way," "those of this way," "the saints," "pilgrims," and "sheep."

Objects of God's Will

One of the most interesting terms used to identify Christians, however, is "the called." It is an unusual topic because many Christians have never been taught the truth about *the called,* a phrase that Paul used in his Epistle to the Romans: "And we know," he said, "that all things work together for good to them that love God, to them who are *the called* according to his purpose. For whom he did foreknow, he also did predestinate to be conformed to the image of his Son, that he might be the firstborn among many brethren. Moreover whom he did predestinate, them he also *called*: and whom *he called*, them he also justified: and whom he justified, them he also glorified" (Romans 8:28–30, emphasis added).

In his commentary on Romans, William R. Newell wrote, "The word 'called' in Romans 8:28 does not mean invited, as we find it in Proverbs. For instance, when we read, 'Unto you, O men, do I call' [Proverbs 8:4]. This would be an appeal to man's will instead of Romans 8:28, which is a description of those who are the objects of God's will, of accomplishing his purpose."[2]

The Mark of the Called

To show how the Gospel of Christ Crucified affected the Jews, Greek pagans, and Christians, Paul said, "We preach Christ crucified,

---

2. William R. Newell, *Romans Verse by Verse* (Chicago: Moody Press), 329.

unto the Jews a stumbling block, and unto the Greeks foolishness; but unto them which *are called*, both Jews and Greeks, Christ the power of God, and the wisdom of God" (1 Corinthians 1:23–24, emphasis added).

In effect, Paul was saying that the mark of the called was neither religious response nor intellectual apprehension. It was their positive acceptance of the Gospel of the crucified Christ because they had been elected by the grace of God. God's electing grace had so marked out the sphere of their being that "the called" was their special name.

They had been called according to God's purposes. If you want to become more familiar with God's purposes and how sinners are called to salvation, take the time to learn the answers to these four questions: 1) What is the purpose of God?, 2) What is the nature of the *two calls?*, 3) Why should we examine our call?; and, 4) Why are some troubled by these important truths?

What Is the Purpose of God?

Not Merely a Desire Expressed

In Romans 8:28 and 30 Paul said that the called were tied into God's purpose and divine predestination. The purpose of God is not merely a desire expressed, but a fixed and all-embracing will that subordinates all things, submerges all opposition, and accomplishes its objective. The dictionary defines "purpose" as "something set up as an object or end to be attained: intention." So we can say that God's purpose is an intelligent decision which he has willed to accomplish.

Prothesis, the Greek word translated as "purpose" in the English Bible, appears twelve times in the New Testament. When used to depict human intention, it shows that man may purpose something but he does not always accomplish the end he intended. God, by his grace, often intervenes in the purposes of men and causes them to fail.

For example, when the crew of a ship on which Paul was a prisoner saw that the south wind was blowing softly they set out for another port and supposed they had obtained their purpose. But a great wind, called *Euroclydon,* caused a fierce storm that wrecked their ship (Acts 27).

When Barnabas visited the church in Antioch and saw how they had been blessed by the grace of God, he exhorted the believers "that with purpose of heart they would cleave unto the Lord" (Acts 11:23).

God's Purpose Is Absolute

Comparing his ministry with that of false teachers, Paul wrote to Timothy and said, "But thou hast fully known my doctrine, manner of life, purpose, faith, longsuffering, charity . . ." (2 Timothy 3:10). Though he carried out his purpose to final victory in finishing his course, he knew that it was by God's grace alone that he could do so. "By the grace of God," he said, "I am what I am" (1 Corinthians 15:10).

God's purpose is absolute, and wholly separate from contingencies. Paul also referred to God's absolute purpose when he wrote about God choosing Jacob over Esau. The twin brothers were not even born, nor had they done any good or evil when their destinies were determined "that the purpose of God according to election might stand, not of works, but of him that calleth" (Romans 9:11). Everything was subordinated to the purpose of God and the end that was predicted was fulfilled with pinpoint accuracy.

God's Purpose Is Eternal

Paul also called God's purpose "the eternal purpose which he purposed in Christ Jesus our Lord" (Ephesians 3:11). Paul shows how certain he was of this when he wrote that God "hath saved us, and called us with an holy calling, not according to our works, but according to his own purpose and grace, which was given us in Christ Jesus before the world began [or before the beginning of time]" (2 Timothy 1:9).

In Romans 8:29–30 Paul explains how God accomplished his purpose for the called. Some people have difficulty with the words "foreknowledge" and "predestination," but those words are not primary in this passage. Instead Paul makes the *purpose of God* its central truth. What is that purpose?

Clearly it is this: From the mass of fallen and sinful humanity, God has chosen and will redeem a company of people to be conformed to the likeness of his Son, Jesus Christ. God loves his Son and has determined to change a great number of people to be like him—not that they become divine; the Bible does not teach that—but rather that they become like Christ in some of his characteristics such as love, joy, peace, holiness, wisdom, patience, grace, faithfulness, and mercy.

Walk on Water?

A story out of India illustrates the contrast between the uncertain, often failing purposes of men and the fixed, determined purpose of God. In 1966, Rao, a Hindu holy man, announced that he would walk on water. His announcement attracted a great deal of attention.

On the day he had chosen to perform his promised feat, a large crowd gathered at the pool in Bombay to witness the event. Rao placed one foot on the surface of the water, but when he placed his other foot on the water he sank beneath its surface. When he emerged from the depths spitting water he looked at the huge crowd of people and shouted, "One of you is an unbeliever!"

Praise God that our salvation has nothing to do with the uncertain purposes of men. Salvation is all of God and he will accomplish the salvation of his elect and the called by his unfailing purpose.

What Is the Nature of the Two Calls?

Communication and Application

Webster's Dictionary defines the word "called" as "a divine summons, a state of being divinely called." While this is likely speaking of the call into the ministry, the Bible teaches that sinners receive *two* calls from God according to his purpose. Jesus indicated the existence of two calls when he said, "Many are called, but few are chosen."

The two calls are part and parcel of God's plan to redeem a people for himself. Election, another essential part of God's plan of salvation, has to do with the purposing and planning of salvation. Vicarious atonement by Christ had to do with the provision of salvation. And the two calls have to do with the communication and application of salvation to elect sinners.

The First Call

The first call is an external, general and ineffective call that invites sinners to come to Christ for salvation. It is an open invitation to all sinners to repent of their sins and turn to Jesus Christ. For example, Jesus said, "Come unto me, all ye that labor and are heavy laden, and I will give you rest" (Matthew 11:28).

He also said, "If anyone would come after me, he must deny himself and take up his cross and follow me" (Matthew 16:24). Standing in the temple teaching the people, Jesus gave this invitation: "If any man thirst, let them come unto me and drink" (John 7:37).

The idea of thirst was also used by Adoniram Judson, missionary to Burma, who amongst other scholarly achievements mastered the Burmese language. He went to the busy marketplace and, speaking in Burmese, invited the people to come to the true God for salvation. He used this invitation from the prophecy of Isaiah: "Ho, everyone that thirsteth, come ye to the waters, and he that hath no money; come ye, buy and eat; yea, come, buy wine and milk without money and without price" (Isaiah 55:1).

In the days of the New Testament Christ and the apostles used the preaching or presentation of the Gospel through personal witnessing to give the general or universal call. The same methods, plus tracts and books, are used today. Every genuine presentation of the Gospel of Jesus Christ is a call for sinners to repent or to forsake their sin and trust in Christ for salvation from their sins. When Paul preached to the Greek philosophers of Athens on Mars Hill he gave a general call when he said, "God commandeth all men everywhere to repent" (Acts 17:30).

Sinners have difficulty with the external, universal, or general call because, being spiritually dead, they cannot make a positive response to it. So it is not only a general, but an ineffective call. They hear the Gospel call and may even understand it up to a point. But they turn away because their love for the pleasures of sin makes the requirements of repentance or forsaking their sins and turning to God undesirable to them. Thus, they may deliberately ignore or neglect the invitation, and turn away.

In Luke 14:16–24, Jesus told the story of those who had been invited to a great supper and refused to attend by giving all kinds of pseudo-reasons that ended with: "I pray thee have me excused." People today still give many false reasons why they should be excused from accepting the invitation of the general call to repent of their sins, believe in Christ, and follow him.

With all the blessings that are offered to them in the Gospel invitation, why do so many refuse to respond favorably? Jesus gave the answer to this question when he said, "And this is the condemnation, that light has come into the world, and men loved darkness rather than light, because their deeds were evil" (John 3:19). Paul too gave the answer when he said, "There is none that understandeth, there is none that seeketh after God" (Romans 3:11).

The Second Call

The total inability of men and women to do anything to save themselves is the reason that they cannot respond in a positive way to the general call. They need help from the Lord. They need a second call that will enable them to accept the Gospel invitation. That is why Jesus said, "No man can come unto me, except the Father which sent me draw him" (John 6:44).

Unlike the general call which is ineffective, the second call is effective, internal, specific, and regenerating. Before creation, God gave a certain number of those he intended to create to his Son Jesus Christ on the proviso that he would go to earth and give his life in sacrifice for their sins.

The second or *effectual* call harvests all those whom God gave to his Son, fulfilling the promise made by Christ when he said, "All that the Father giveth to me shall come to me" (John 6:37).

"The word *called*," said Dr. C. D. Cole, "is never in any of the epistles applied to those who are the recipients of a mere external invitation to the Gospel. It always signifies an inward and effectual call, that brings [one] to Christ and salvation."[3]

Paul did not address his Epistle to the Romans, which is the great biblical treatise on salvation, to every Roman citizen. He addressed it to those who are referred to as "the called of Jesus Christ" (Romans 1:6). Later he made a forceful, assuring statement about the second call: "God's gifts and his call," he said, "are irrevocable . . ." (Romans 11:29, NIV).

We have learned so far why the general call is ineffective and does not move sinners to make a positive response. Why is it, then, that the second, *internal* or specific call made to sinners, is so effective and brings those who receive it to salvation?

The answer is that it is an internal work of God the Holy Spirit. It is God who predestinates, calls, justifies, and glorifies elect sinners. The personal pronoun "he," referring to God, is used six times in this statement by Paul: "Moreover whom he did predestinate, them he also called: and whom he called, them he also justified: and whom he justified, them he also glorified" (Romans 8:30). Commenting on this verse, William R Newell explained it this way:

---

3. Dr. Claude Duval Cole was a Baptist pastor, seminary professor, and author of the three-volume work *Definitions of Doctrine*.

Do not argue about man's decision or *whosoever will* here. They may be found in other places in the Bible, but here we are being told that salvation is connected with the Almighty God of the Universe and it cannot fail for he is sovereign.

This is the reason that Paul in the book of Romans, three chapters later, says, "O the depth of the riches both of the wisdom and knowledge of God! How unsearchable are his judgments, and his ways past finding out" (Romans 11:33).

The second or inward call upon the elect sinner is effective because the Holy Spirit takes the spoken or written Gospel and uses it to open the sinner's heart and regenerate him. By this operation, he provides the sinner with a new spiritual life that, in turn, gives him an understanding of the Gospel and the desire, ability and will to repent of his sins and to believe in Jesus Christ.

A sinner without this new birth cannot know or receive the things of the Spirit of God because they are foolishness unto him. The sinner who has been born again, however, understands and receives them with gladness because his new spiritual life has given him spiritual discernment.

A biblical example of how the second call works is given in the story of a woman named Lydia, a dealer in purple cloth from the city of Thyatira who was a worshiper of God. Though she had never even so much as heard of the Gospel in the first decades of her life, the Lord opened her heart to respond to Paul's message (Acts 16:14).

The second call is a divine call that can be made only by the Godhead. The story of Christ's raising of Lazarus from the dead is a case in point. Those people who stood around his sepulcher could have yelled, "Lazarus, come forth" until they ran out of voice-power and nothing would have happened. But when Jesus, who is the Resurrection and the Life, said, "Lazarus come forth," the dead man obeyed his divine call and came forth risen from the dead!

This is a good picture of what happens when an elect sinner hears the general call of the Gospel and the Spirit calls him internally and effectively. He rises from his spiritual death, repents of his sins, believes in Christ as his Lord and Saviour, and goes forth to follow him.

Some teach that one is born again by believing in Jesus, but God's *ordo salutis* or order of salvation clearly proves that the new birth comes before repentance and faith, which are the result, not the cause, of the new birth. If it were otherwise, salvation would depend upon the sinner and his ability, which concept Paul thoroughly refutes in Romans 8:28–30, quoted above.

WHY SHOULD WE EXAMINE OUR CALL?

Make Your Calling Sure

Each of us should ask himself this life-and-death question: "Am *I* one of the called?" He should ask it because every person who professes faith in Christ should be able to say, "I know I am among the number of those who are the called according to God's purpose."

The apostles of Christ taught believers to examine themselves to make sure they were genuine Christians. "Examine yourselves," said Paul, "whether ye be in the faith; prove your own selves. Know ye not your own selves, how that Jesus Christ is in you, except ye be reprobates" (2 Corinthians 13:5).

In effect Paul was saying that Christians should make sure they have been truly called and born again by God the Holy Spirit because only by that call can one enjoy the gift of faith in Christ. It's a message that still applies to us today.

After Peter the apostle told his readers to add to their faith virtue, knowledge, self-control, perseverance, godliness, brotherly kindness, and love, he said this: "But he that lacketh these things is blind, and cannot see afar off, and hath forgotten that he was purged from his old sins. Wherefore the rather, brethren, give diligence to make your calling and election sure: for if ye do these things, ye shall never fail" (2 Peter 1:5–10). The practice of those seven character-building traits is evidence that one's calling and election are sure.

Stony and Thorny Ground

Many are deceived into thinking that because they responded to an outward call, they are saved and have the inward call. Jesus warned against this deception in his explanation of his parable of "The Sower and the Good Seed." In this parable, he spoke of seed falling on stony ground where it sprang up but soon withered away because there was no room for it to take root. He also spoke of seed falling amongst thorns. Explaining the meaning of his parable he said:

> But he that received the seed into stony places, the same is he that heareth the word, and anon with joy receiveth it. Yet hath he not root in himself, but dureth for a while: for when tribulation or persecution ariseth because of the word, by and by he is offended. He also that received seed among thorns is he that heareth the word; and the care of this world, and the deceitfulness of riches, choke the word and he becometh unfruitful. (Matthew 13:20–22)

Thousands have been deceived into believing they were saved by an emotional experience at an evangelistic crusade. They responded to an outward call from the evangelist, went forward to the platform, shook hands with the preacher and thought that by doing those things they had received the salvation of the Bible. In many cases they were *stony ground* or *thorny ground* hearers.

All Who Hear Are Not Called

"If men heed no more than the outward call," said the late Dr. Donald Grey Barnhouse, "they become members of the visible church. If the inward call is heard in our hearts, we become members of the invisible church. The first call will unite us merely to a group of professing members; but the inward call unites us to Christ himself, and to all that have been born again.

"The outward call may bring with it certain intellectual knowledge of the truth; the inward call brings us the faith of the heart, the hope that anchors us forever to the Son of God and to the love that must ever draw us to him who first loved us. The outward call many times ends in formalism, the inward call in true life. The outward call may curb the tendencies of the old nature and keep a soul in outward morality; the inward call will cure the plague that is in us and bring us to triumph in Christ."[4]

The Bible says that a regenerating call to salvation originates with the triune God, who also carries it to completion. The natural man does not respond to God on the basis of the general call alone. But that does not mean that the general call is not necessary. God makes the specific or effectual call, usually through the general call. Through the preaching of the Gospel by evangelists, ministers, and missionaries, and the explanation of the Gospel by lay Christians, God gives the effectual call to elect sinners.

The Bible teaches that God does not *call* everyone who hears the Gospel. Men sow the seed broadly. Some of it will fall by the wayside, some on stony or shallow ground, other among thorns, but some does fall on *good ground.* Good ground was used by Christ to represent the heart of man that has been prepared by God to receive the Gospel seed. When the Gospel seed enters a heart prepared by God, the Giver of Life, he blesses the sowing, causes the seed to take root, and produces a spiritual harvest. When a sinner is saved it includes all five links of what Bible scholars call "the golden chain of redemption." The links in that chain are foreknowledge, predestination, calling, justification, and glorification.

It Is the Same Today

Here's another way of looking at the two calls: Since God usually calls effectively through the general call, it is imperative that a general call be given. Men are not saved by the call, but by the triune God— Father, Son, and Holy Spirit. Theologians say that God the Father

---

4. The late Dr. Donald Grey Barnhouse was the minister of a large Presbyterian church in Philadelphia, a radio and television speaker, and a giant among conservative Presbyterian ministers.

planned redemption, God the Son accomplished redemption, and God the Holy Spirit applies redemption to elect sinners.

One must have a new spiritual life in order to enter the spiritual kingdom of God. That is the reason that Jesus told Nicodemus, a learned religious leader, that one must be born again to see and to enter the kingdom of heaven. When Jesus began his ministry, he received much opposition. "He was in the world, and the world was made by him, and the world knew him not. He came unto his own, and his own received him not" (John 1:10–11).

It is the same today: the unbelieving people of this world have no desire to know or receive him. They sneer at the preaching of the Gospel and label it foolishness. Yet, the Bible says that "It pleased God by the foolishness of preaching to save them that believe" (1 Corinthians 1:21).

No one but God could invent a way of saving sinful men and women. The secret is that the work of effectively calling sinners to Christ for salvation is all of God. In his sovereignty, however. God uses human instruments to scatter the seed of his redemptive truth.

WHY ARE SOME TROUBLED
BY THESE IMPORTANT TRUTHS?

One Can Know If He Is of the Elect

Many people get bogged down or hung up on the great biblical subjects of God's foreknowledge, predestination, and election. "If these doctrines are true," they say, "then there is nothing we can do."

Another says, "If I have been elected I'll be saved; if not, I'll be lost. My fate is fixed, so why should I worry about it?" One will ask, "How can I know if I am one of God's elect?" Another says, "If I am not one of God's elect sheep there is no hope for me." What can we say to these?

John Bunyan, author of *Pilgrim's Progress,* was so troubled by these things that he went into a deep state of despair. But there is no reason for such despondency over these great truths. We can know we are of the elect if we have responded to the Gospel by answering God's call to repent and believe.

How do we know that Abraham was of the elect? He responded when God called him to leave Ur of the Chaldees and go to a land that he would afterwards inherit. Abraham obeyed and went, even though he did not know where he was going. He did know, however, who had sent him.

It was the same with Moses. We know he was predestinated to be saved because he chose to share the oppression of God's people instead of enjoying the fleeting pleasures of sin (Hebrews 11:25).

How do we know that Saul of Tarsus, the vicious persecutor of Christians, was elected? His very life of apostolic service to Christ after his conversion on the road to Damascus is evidence that he "was not disobedient to that heavenly vision" (Acts 26:19). In his apostolic writings he said that he had not chosen God, but God had chosen him, had mercy upon him, forgave him of his sins, and gave him eternal life.

How can you and I know if we are of the elect? There is only one way and it is not by trying to peer into the counsels of God and stripping the cover from the book of divine foreknowledge and predestination. The only way we can know that God has chosen us to be saved is that we have responded to the gospel with sincere repentance and genuine faith in Christ that leads us to live for him.

Election No Hinderance to Salvation

Though predestination and election are divine truths, they do not prevent sinners from being saved. Sinners do not go to hell because they were not elected. They go to hell because they are guilty sinners who refuse to believe. Paul said, "Believe on the Lord Jesus Christ and thou shalt be saved" (Acts 16:31). And John the apostle wrote, "As many as received him, to them gave he power [or authority] to become the sons of God, even to them that believe on his name" (John 1:12). If we have heeded the call, if we truly believe in Christ, if we have received him by faith, then we can know that God has set his love upon us and chosen us from before the foundation of the world.

Election does not prevent anyone from repenting and believing or from being saved because everyone who repents and believes will be saved. "God has promised forgiveness for your repentance," said Augustine; "God has not promised tomorrow for your procrastination."

The Bible clearly teaches that so far as salvation is concerned man suffers from total inability. But it also teaches that man is responsible. One of the great truths I learned in my theological studies was this: "Inability does not cancel responsibility."

Some argue that it is not fair that a man cannot come to Christ unless God draws him and God should not have to give an effective call. I'll respond to that as Paul often did—with a question: "Was it right for God to give the Ten Commandments when he knew that no one could keep them?"

The Lord Has Done It

Most of us do not know how the effective call of God can give us peace, hope, and assurance at the loss of a loved one—one of the most trying and critical times of life. The story of Jonathan and Sarah Edwards is a case in point. Ministering to a church in Stockridge, Massachusetts, Edwards was a renowned preacher in the Great Awakening revival of the Eighteenth century and was America's leading theologian. Dr. D. Martyn Lloyd Jones has this to say about him:

> No man is more relevant to the present conditions of Christianity than Jonathan Edwards. . . . He was a mighty theologian and a great evangelist at the same time. . . . He was preeminently the theologian of revival. If you want to know anything about true revival, Edwards is the man to consult . . . My advice is, read Jonathan Edwards. Go back to something solid and deep and real.[5]

---

5. From *The Puritan Experiment in the New World,* The Westminster Conference Papers, 1976, p. 103.

Jonathan Edwards had just been appointed president of the College of New Jersey, now known as Princeton University, when he died as a result of being vaccinated against smallpox. He was only fifty-four years old. He left his wife, Sarah, and ten children. Iain Murray gives this account of Mrs. Edwards' reaction:

When the news reached Stockridge Sarah Edwards was suffering so much from rheumatism in her neck that she could scarcely hold a pen, but brief lines written to [her daughter] Esther on April 3 epitomize the spirit in which she sought to live with her husband for more than thirty years:

What shall I say? A holy and good God has covered us with a dark cloud. O that we may kiss the rod, and lay our hands upon our mouths! The Lord has done it. He has made us adore his goodness, that we had him so long. But my God lives; and he has my heart. O what a legacy my husband, and your father, has left us! We are all given to God, and there I am, and love to be.[6]

What a letter! What a triumph for one of "the called of God according to his purpose!" (Romans 8:28)

---

6. Iain Murray, *Jonathan Edwards: A New Biography* (Edinburgh: Banner of Truth Trust, 1987), 442.

CHAPTER NINE

Perfect Communion

What we call the Lord's Prayer was not a prayer that Christ used, but a model prayer that he taught to his disciples. The real Lord's Prayer is recorded in John 17—a passage often described as the holy of holies of the New Testament. In that prayer our Lord Jesus seems to overleap the Cross, and permits us to hear him communing with his Father as from the other side of the rent veil.

Nothing Like It

"The Seventeenth Chapter of John," said Bishop John Ryle, "is the most remarkable in the Bible. It stands alone, and there is nothing like it."

Our English Bible uses the words, "I pray," three times in John 17. The Greek in the original, however, is never used about man praying to God. It is a verb signifying, "making request on the plane of an equal." This is something that is so high above and beyond what man calls praying that the prayer of John 17 should be called "The Lord's Perfect Communion with His Father."

In this prayer, Christ did not petition the Father, but rather stood on the ground of divine equality and presented august desires that met with immediate response in that relationship of perfect oneness within the Godhead.

"This," said Martin Luther, "is truly beyond measure, a warm and hearty prayer. He opens the depths of his heart, both in reference to us and to his Father, and he pours them all out. It sounds so honest, so simple; it is so deep, so rich, so wide, no one can fathom it."

Three Distinct Movements

The high level of the Lord's Prayer in John 17 makes it an unusual topic. The chapter's high level of quality was also recognized by Martin Luther's friend and fellow Reformer, Philip Melanchton. While giving the last lecture prior to his death he said of it, "There is no voice which has ever been heard, either in heaven or in earth, more exalted, more holy, more fruitful, more sublime, than the prayer offered up by the Son of God himself."

The communion of this great prayer in John 17 flows in three distinct movements. Verses one to five deal with the Lord Jesus. In verses 6 through 19, Christ prays for the disciples living at that time. And in verses 20 through 26, he prays for those elect sinners who shall believe in the future. If you would like to know more about this wonderful prayer, join me as together we try to increase our understanding of the four subjects germane to the Lord's High priestly prayer of John 17: 1) The Saviour's Glorification; 2) The Saints' Preservation; 3) The Believer's Sanctification; and, 4) The Christian's Joy.

THE SAVIOUR'S GLORIFICATION

"The hour is come . . ."

Heaven was as near to the soul of the Lord Jesus Christ as the spoken name *Father*. Six times in this chapter Christ addresses God—not a God that is afar off, but the God with whom the Son was holding immediate and intimate communion—in perfect union, understanding, purpose, and will. John's record of Christ's high priestly prayer begins:

These words spake Jesus, and lifted up his eyes to heaven, and said, Father, the hour is come; glorify thy Son, that thy Son also may glorify thee: As thou hast given him power over all flesh, that he should give eternal life to as many as thou hast given him. And this is life eternal, that they might know thee the only true God, and Jesus Christ, whom thou hast sent. (John 17:1–3)

The occasion of this great high priestly prayer was not something distant and uncertain, but an event long anticipated that had arrived. "The hour is come," said Christ. God had appointed "the hour" of his Son's sacrificial death before he created the world. The divine purpose was centered on it and all the threads of history converged upon that event. Yes, "the hour had come" with all of its darkness, anguish, and humiliation.

Glorify Thy Son

Standing on the threshold of his imminent sacrifice of himself for sinners, how did Christ pray? Did he ask his Father to deliver him? *No.* Did he ask for personal sustenance? *No.*

He prayed, "Glorify thy Son."

Such a request would be altogether inappropriate for anyone else but Jesus to pray under any circumstances because glory belongs exclusively to the Godhead. In contrast, we approach the same Father and pray saying, "Give us, forgive us, lead us, and deliver us," but we never ask God to glorify us. Instead, we ascribe all glory to him. "For thine," we pray, "is the kingdom and the power and the glory."

The prayer that Christ taught his disciples to pray carried with it a confession of utter dependence upon God's grace. As redeemed sinners we can readily see that appropriate words for us to use in prayer would be these: "Give us, for we are poor and must draw upon thy wealth. Be merciful unto us and forgive us, because we are sinful. Lead us, for we are foolish sheep who have gone astray. Deliver us, for we are weak and must lean on thy strength."

Difference in Prayers

What a difference there was between the prayer of King Saul and the prayer of King David! "I have sinned," said Saul, "yet honor me now I pray thee" (1 Samuel 15:30). This was the prayer of a reprobate and it is no wonder that he plunged more deeply into shame and darkness following it.

Going against God's revealed will, Saul sought advice from the witch of Endor. He ended his slide into wickedness by committing suicide. David, however, who knew how to pray, looked to God in Psalm 51, saying this:

> Have mercy upon me, O God,
> According to thy lovingkindness:
> According to the multitude of thy tender mercies
> Blot out my transgressions:
> Wash me thoroughly from mine iniquity,
> And cleanse me from my sin.
> For I acknowledge my transgressions:
> And my sin is ever before me.
> Against thee, thee only have I sinned,
> And done this evil in thy sight:
> That thou mightest be justified when thou speakest,
> And be clear when thou judgest.

Though David humbled himself before the Lord and exalted God, he himself was exalted to become the royal ancestor of the Messiah. With all of his exaltation, however, David was still a sinner and could not pray as the sinless Saviour prayed. Only Christ the equal and eternal Son of God had the right to ask God the Father to glorify him 1) in his sufferings and, 2) after he had suffered, by accomplishing the task he had been sent to do—the redemption of his elect people.

Without One Dash of Repentance

God answered Christ's prayer by sending an angel to strengthen him in the Garden, by Pilate's statement at Jesus' trial: "I find no fault in him" (Luke 23:14), and by the remarkable salvation of the dying thief on the Cross (Luke 23: 43).

Jesus was also glorified by the veil rent in the temple at the moment of his death and by the confession of the Roman centurion who, looking at Christ on the Cross, said, "Truly this was the Son of God" (Matthew 27:54). Most of all, he was glorified in his triumphant Resurrection and in his exaltation to the right hand of the Father in heaven. These glorifications represent the bedrock of our faith.

Bowing in the presence of the Lord, most Christians begin a life of piety with tears of contrition and repentance. "In Christ," however, as one preacher put it, "you have piety without one dash of repentance." He had no failures to confess and he never wept over his sins because he had none.

"I have glorified thee on the earth," he prayed, "I have finished the work which thou gavest me to do. And now, O Father, glorify thou me with thine own self with the glory which I had with thee before the world was" (John 17:4–5).

Because of the wonderful life he had already lived on earth, he could ask for what was rightly his: the glorification that he had with his Father before his Incarnation; yea, before the foundation of the world.

The Finished Work

When Christ said, "I have finished the work which thou gavest me to do," it appears that he was speaking as though his Calvary experience was over. Some interpret him as meaning that he had finished the work of living a sinless human life by which he earned the righteousness to be imputed to his elect people. They support this view by pointing to the fact that Jesus put these two statements together as though they were related: "I have glorified thee on the earth: I have finished the work which thou gavest me to do." They also say that Jesus was speaking of his work of dying on the Cross when he said, "It is finished." In other words, he was speaking first of the work of his victorious life and second of the work of his vicarious death—the two aspects of his mission.

His great condescension reminds us of Peter the Great, who laid aside his royal robes to become a laborer in a shipyard. He wanted to learn how to build ships so that Russia could have a navy. The Lord Jesus Christ, whose royal position was infinitely higher than that of Peter the Great, laid aside his heavenly glory for a few years to become the Good Shepherd on earth in order to accomplish redemption for his sheep.

Since Christ and his people enjoy a special union, his glorification cannot be separated from them. "And all mine are thine," prayed Jesus, "and thine are mine; and I am glorified in them" (John 17:10). Having studied his glorification, let us turn now to another matter . . .

The Saints' Preservation

Same Doctrines as Calvin Taught

As believers, we should not only revel in the glorification of Jesus Christ, but we should be thrilled over what he says and prays about us. This is the reason that John Knox, the eminent Scottish Reformer, had John 17 read to him *every* day during his final illness. Those precious words of our Lord's Prayer consoled and strengthened him as he left his beloved Scotland to go to heaven.

This is another chapter of God's Word that does not sit too well with those of the Arminian persuasion. John 17 has the five points of Calvinism, as does John 6 and John 10. The five points are these: 1) Total inability or depravity; 2) unconditional election; 3) particular redemption; 4) irresistible grace; and, 5) the perseverance of the saints.

He Shall See and Be Satisfied

Seven times in John 17 the Lord refers to believers as having been given to God the Son by God the Father. Part of the Son's glorification was his securing the salvation and preservation of those elect sinners. Part of Christ's appointed mission was to give eternal life to all of the elect. "As thou hast given him power over all flesh," said Christ, "that he should give eternal life to as many as thou hast given him" (John 17:2).

In his eternal counsels, the Father had appointed the Son to save a certain number of persons in the human race and to conduct them to glory. This verse distinguishes between Christ's universal authority "over all flesh" and his narrower charge—"as many as thou has given him." The story of Joseph in Egypt is an illustration of this. He was given authority over all Egypt, but his own brethren had a special claim upon his affections. According to the Bible, God gave the elect to Christ as *a reward*. The prophet explained this when he wrote,

> He shall see of the travail of his soul, and shall be satisfied: by his knowledge shall my righteous servant justify many, for he shall bear their iniquities. Therefore will I divide him a portion with the great, and he shall divide the spoil with the strong; because he hath poured out his soul unto death: and he was numbered with the transgressors; and he bare the sin of many, and made intercession for the transgressors. (Isaiah 53:11–12)

Chain of Redemption

When the Jewish mob and Judas came to take Jesus, he asked them who they were looking for and they said, "Jesus." Jesus then told them that he was the one they sought. "I have told you I am he," he said: "If therefore ye seek me, let these [meaning his disciples] go their way: that the saying might be fulfilled which he spake, 'Of them which thou gavest me have I lost none'" (John 18:8–9).

According to John 17:6, believers, by foreordination, were the Father's. The Father chose them, the Son redeemed them, and the Spirit quickens them. Their election is known by their interest in Christ—an interest they received at their new birth. All who are of God's flock are put into Christ's hands and he sent his Holy Spirit to care for them. Peter emphasized this truth when he spoke of those who were "Elect according to the foreknowledge of God the Father, through sanctification of the Spirit, unto obedience and sprinkling of the blood of Jesus Christ" (1 Peter 1:2).

God's Word contains a wonderful chain of redemption. It comes from the Father, is dispensed by the Son, and is applied by the Spirit. Having come from the Father, redemption is conveyed or mediated to us through Christ by the Spirit. Not one of the elect will be lost because if one were lost the glory of Christ the Perfect Servant would be tarnished forever.

"I pray not for the world . . ."

The doctrine of particular redemption—that Christ died to save only his people, the elect—was clearly stated by Christ when he said, "I pray for them: I pray not for the world, but for them which thou hast given me; for they are thine" (John 17:9). The advocates of universal redemption, who say that Christ died for everybody in the whole world, have a difficult time with this verse because Christ said he did not pray for the world. It would be a strange thing for Christ not to pray for the whole world if he died for the whole world, as the universalists claim.

Writing about John 17, John Gill, a predecessor of Charles Spurgeon, said, "For whom Christ is the propitiation, he is an advocate; and for whom he died, he makes intercession, and for no others in a spiritual way."

"I kept them in thy name."

In his apostolic band, Jesus had two men named Judas—Judas Iscariot, who betrayed him, and another Judas, of whom little is said. In fact, the only reference to him is in John 14:22, where the lesser-known Judas is recorded as asking this question of Jesus: "Lord, how is it that thou wilt manifest thyself to us, and not unto the world?" Here is another passage that points to the doctrine of particular redemption—the difference between Christ's relationship to believers and his relationship to unbelievers.

Christ made a tremendous statement on the preservation or security of the saints when he said, "While I was with them in the world, I kept them in thy name: those that thou gavest me I have kept, and none of them is lost, but the son of perdition; that the scripture might be fulfilled" (John 17:12).

A stable hand looking after the famous racing horse Man of War in Kentucky was a Baptist deacon. One day he struck up a conversation with the preacher, writer, and theologian John Macauly, who had come to see the famous horse.

"There is never a minute, day or night," he said, "that this horse is without a human eye upon him." If that was true of men and a horse, how much more must it be true of our heavenly Father who keeps his eye upon his own!

Few Hymns on Election

Most of our hymns center on our admiration, love, worship, and the things we do or desire to do concerning our relationship to God. For example, we sing, "Blessed Assurance," "A Child of the King," "All to Jesus I Surrender," "Am I a Soldier of the Cross," "Crown Him with Many Crowns," and many others. But few hymns speak of God's concern over his elect. Here is one of them:

> When I feel my faith will fail,
> He will hold me fast;
> When the tempter would prevail,
> He will hold me fast.
>
> I could never keep my hold,
> He must hold me fast;

For my love is often cold,
He will hold me fast.

I am precious in his sight,
He will hold me fast;
Those he saves are his delight,
He will hold me fast.

He will not let my soul be lost,
He will hold me fast;
Bought by him at such a cost,
He will hold me fast.

The Believer's Sanctification

They Belong Together

Though clearly taught throughout the Word of God, no doctrine has been so misunderstood and subject to misinterpretation than the doctrine of sanctification. In his high priestly prayer for his elect people Jesus said, "Sanctify them through thy truth: thy word is truth. . . . And for their sakes I sanctify myself, that they also might be sanctified through the truth" (John 17:17,19).

One of the major errors being taught about sanctification is that it can be separated from justification. We find this error in the "no-Lordship Gospel" taught by Charles Ryrie in his book *So Great Salvation* and by Zane Hodges in his book *Absolutely Free!*

Campus Crusade also promotes a wrong view of sanctification in its carnal Christian doctrines. They teach that one can be saved by believing in Christ as Saviour without acknowledging him as their Lord.

For example, in his book, Ryrie says, "No turning from sin is required for salvation," (p. 99), and Hodges, in his book, says, "Calling on the Lord means *appealing* to him, not *submitting* to him" (pp. 193–195, his emphasis).

Campus Crusade tracts on the carnal Christian teach that there are three classes of humanity: unsaved people; spiritual Christians, and carnal Christians. Lewis Sperry Chafer made this view popular back in 1918 in his book, *He That Is Spiritual*. It also appeared in the notes of *The Scofield Reference Bible*. John F. MacArthur, Jr. describes this erroneous teaching:

> The Campus Crusade literature features a diagram with three circles representing the three classes of humanity. At the center of each circle is a throne. The non-Christian has self on the throne with Christ outside the circle. The carnal Christian has "invited" Christ into the circle but keeps self enthroned. The spiritual Christian puts Christ on the throne, with self at the foot of the throne. The tract challenges carnal Christians to become spiritual. Millions of these pamphlets have been distributed worldwide over the past thirty years or so. They are undoubtedly the most widely read single bit of no-Lordship literature and have helped influence multitudes to accept the carnal-spiritual Christian dichotomy as biblical.[1]

What Can We Do?

Knowing there is so much misunderstanding and misinterpretation of this important doctrine, what can we do to avoid being led astray from the biblical position on sanctification? First, we can make sure that we understand that sanctification is rightly related to all other doctrines.

Second, we must avoid trying to interpret sanctification by our experiences.

Third, we should accept the truth that a right understanding of sanctification depends upon a careful consideration of all the scripture passages bearing on sanctification.

---

1. John F. MacArthur, Jr., *Faith Works: The Gospel According to the Apostles* (Dallas Word Publishing, 1993), 125

Set Apart for Holy Use

The word, "sanctify," has this one uniform meaning throughout the Scriptures: "to set apart by God for his holy use." When Christ said, "For their sake I sanctify myself" (John 17:19), he must have meant that for their sake he set himself apart. The word never has reference, as some claim, to inward cleansing, still less to the eradication of the old human nature.

According to the Bible, believers are sanctified by the Holy Spirit (Romans 15:16), by the will of God (Hebrews 10:10), by the Blood of Christ (Hebrews 13:13), by the Word of truth (John 17:17), by faith in Christ (Acts 26:18), and by God the Father (Jude 1).

Election is sanctification by the Father. Redemption *accomplished* is sanctification by the Son. And regeneration is sanctification by the Holy Spirit. These three are positional and absolute, admitting of no degrees and unconcerned with any gradual process. In each case the sanctification or setting apart for holy use is complete and final. When Christ said, "Sanctify them with thy truth," however, he was speaking of the other aspect of sanctification—its practical and progressive application of the truth of the Word of God. "Thy word is truth," he said.

Three Dangers Survived

Everything we believe and do and say is to be tested by the Word of God. By it we should strive to formulate our thoughts and regulate our conduct. Since God's Word is truth that will never change, we should place a very high value upon its doctrines, precepts, and exhortations. The Bible is a survivor par excellence because, as one unknown author has said, "This deathless book has survived three great dangers: the negligence of its friends; the false systems built upon it; and the warfare of those who hated it."

Down through the centuries the Bible has withstood the onslaughts and attacks of the severest nature. In every age, blinded by their prejudice and governed by their passions, evil men, like King

Jehoiakim, have tried to cut it to pieces or to destroy it by burning (Jeremiah 36).

The Bible, however, like God its Author, is eternal—it will never die! It is a "tried stone laid in Zion" that will survive every storm unscathed. Its eternal message will abide though heaven and earth should pass away. Since it is by his Word that God sanctifies us, how dearly we should treasure it! We should steer clear of those people who deny any part of the Bible . . . as we would a deadly epidemic or a poisonous rattlesnake.

"He that hath ears," said Jesus, "let him hear." He also said, "Take heed therefore how ye hear" (Luke 8:8,18).

THE CHRISTIAN'S JOY

A Joy No Man Can Take

Happiness and joy are not synonyms. In fact, there is a great deal of difference between them. "Happiness" comes from the old English word "hap" and has to do with chance happenings. If conditions or happenings are pleasant, the unbeliever is happy, but if they are unpleasant, he is unhappy. The man with genuine faith in Christ, however, has a deep-toned joy as he walks in fellowship with God. No happenings or conditions can affect or remove true Christian joy, for Jesus said, "Your heart shall rejoice, and your joy no man taketh from you" (John 16:22).

It was such joy that gave power to the testimony of the early disciples in the face of vicious opposition. Men beat them, put them in prison, fastened their feet in stocks, and condemned them to death. But they took it all—and with songs of praise to God on their lips.

For example, after the apostles had been beaten by the Jewish Sanhedrin for preaching in the name of Jesus, they left the place of torture "rejoicing that they were counted worthy to suffer shame for his name. And daily in the temple, and in every house, they ceased not to teach and preach Jesus Christ" (Acts 5:41–42).

Paul and Silas were arrested in Philippi for preaching the Gospel and for casting an evil spirit out of a young woman. After laying many painful stripes upon them, the authorities put them into an inner dungeon and made their feet fast in the stocks. But the excruciating pain and the seemingly hopeless situation did not make them downhearted. Filled with the joy of the Lord that no man could take from them, they "prayed, and sang praises unto God" (Acts 16:23–25).

"Joyless Christian" Is a Self-Contradiction

Such joy is not of the world for it is the manifest joy of the Lord that only he can give. In the Upper Room, Jesus celebrated the Passover with his disciples and told them many things that they were later to remember. Although he knew that shortly he was to be tried and sentenced to death by crucifixion, he said: "These things have I spoken unto you, that my joy might remain in you, and that your joy might be full" (John 15:11).

In the light of all this, a miserable, joyless Christian is a self-contradiction. He is out of communion with the Father. He has allowed his heart and his life to be taken up with other interests. Consequently he no longer walks in the light of God's countenance. Perhaps you are a believer who could be described as miserable and joyless. If so, what should you do about it?

What Is the Remedy?

First confess your sins and ask God to forgive you. Second, put away anything in your life that hinders communion with your heavenly Father. Third, make regular use of the means of grace that God has provided for the maintenance of your joy in the Lord: The Word of truth, prayer, meditation, daily occupation of the heart with the Lord Jesus, church attendance, Christian fellowship, witnessing for Christ. Also, dwell constantly on your living hope or, as John Calvin called it, "the priceless treasure of a future life with Christ."

In this chaotic world, people visiting foreign countries flee to their own country's embassy for protection and safety when they are in trouble. The great high priestly prayer of the Lord Jesus, as recorded in John 17, is the believer's embassy. Like John Knox, we can find safety, protection, and refreshment by a study of its twenty-six verses.

CHAPTER TEN

The Mystery
of David's Tabernacle

After Simon Peter told the Council at Jerusalem how God had revealed that he was taking a people for himself from among the Gentiles, James, the half brother of Christ, stood up to speak. He said that the prophets of the Old Testament agreed with Peter. Then he quoted from the prophecy of Amos, where the Lord made this prediction:

> After this I will return, and will build again the tabernacle of David, which is fallen down; and I will build again the ruins thereof, and I will set it up: That the residue of men might seek after the Lord, and all the Gentiles, upon *whom* my name is called, saith the Lord, *who* doeth all these things. (Acts 15:16–17)

When we think of the tabernacle, most of us think of the one Moses set up in the wilderness, which ultimately was replaced by the temple that Solomon built. Knowing that God refused to allow David to build the temple, it comes as a mystery to us as to what the Lord meant by his prediction about building again the tabernacle of David that had fallen down. This is an unusual topic because it is still a mystery to most Christians.

Would you like to clear up some of that mystery and gain a better understanding of the meaning of the tabernacle of David? I found that the subject had to be studied in the light of God's plan to redeem a people for himself. With that in mind I am going to use this chapter to make some suggestions germane to the subject that should help us to solve the mystery.

Reject the Popular View

For many years one view or interpretation of this passage has been so popular it has dominated the evangelical scene. That interpretation is the dispensational idea that in it the Lord predicted or prophesied the rebuilding of the physical temple of Jerusalem that was destroyed in A.D. 70. This prophecy, say dispensationalists, is yet to be fulfilled. When it is built, they say, the Lord Jesus will come and set up his throne in the temple and will visibly rule the peoples of the earth. They also teach that millions will journey to Jerusalem to worship the Lord on his earthly "throne of David."

In his 1917 edition *of The Scofield Reference Bible,* C. I. Scofield said this about Acts 15:16: "Dispensationally, this is the most important passage in the New Testament." In his 1967 edition, he said, "This important passage shows God's program for this age. The rebuilding of David's tabernacle is none other than the temple and is in the future. The Amos passage predicts the blessing of the Gentiles after the rebuilding of the tabernacle of David."

Without questioning the sincerity of Scofield, we must ask. Was his interpretation of Acts 15:16 correct? Does the passage in Acts 15 or in Amos 9, from which James quoted in his address to the Council in Jerusalem, even hint at the idea that the ancient temple will be rebuilt in Jerusalem? According to a thorough examination of the text, the answer is "no" to each question.

It seems to me that God meant something quite different from what *The Scofield Reference Bible* and the school of dispen-sationalism teach. I am convinced that in his prediction of Acts 15:16–17 the

Lord had something infinitely more glorious and blessed in mind—something eternal that could not be spoiled or ended.

Most Christians interpret the words, "After this I will return," as predicting a future second coming of Christ that has not yet come to pass. But a study of both Amos nine and Acts 15 shows that they have nothing to say about a future second coming of Christ.

"I will return" is an English translation of the Greek word *anastrepho*, which has no Hebrew equivalent in Amos 9. When James used that phrase he was indicating the context of the passage in Amos rather than any words within it. The previous verses spoke of God's judgment upon his people—that he will not utterly destroy them. The Lord said that after that time of judgment he would turn again to his people and bless them by rebuilding David's tabernacle and by their possessing the Gentile nations round about them.

Evidently James saw the rebuilding of David's tabernacle as pointing to the blessing of the Jews through faith in Christ and the possession of the Gentiles pointing to their salvation through the Gospel. The word "return" of Acts 15:16 does not refer to a future second coming of Christ, but God turning again to his people to bless them after he had judged and punished them. The building again of the ruins means the raising up again of David's house.

Six different Greek words are used in the New Testament with reference to Christ's second coming, but *anastrepho*, used in Acts 15:16, is not among them. It means "to turn about" and is used repeatedly with respect to how one behaves or walks or conducts himself. This meaning fits the statement made in Amos 9 and Acts 15.

If the popular view of Acts 15 is the correct interpretation and the rebuilding of David's tabernacle is yet to come in the future, the words of the Lord in Amos quoted by James would have no bearing on the problem that faced the first church council.

Check the Historical Background

In 1 Samuel 7:11–16, God gave a revelation to Nathan the prophet for David that included an irrefutable clue as to the meaning of the prophecy by Amos. He told David that he would have a descendant who would build a house for the Lord's name. This was fulfilled in Solomon, who built the great temple in Jerusalem. He also told David that he would have another descendant who would have an everlasting kingdom, house, and throne. "He shall build an house for my name," said the Lord, "and I will establish the throne of his kingdom forever."

What was this house? By the very nature of the case it could not have been the stone temple that Solomon had erected in Jerusalem. Instead, the Lord revealed in seed form what the house was going to be. And let them make me a sanctuary," he said; "that I may dwell among them" (Exodus 25:8).

That sanctuary was the tabernacle that Moses built. It was used for many years by Israel, who recognized it as the dwelling place of God. Especially was that true of the mercy seat on the Ark of the Covenant between the cherubim, where shone the radiant, visible, uncreated light—the Shekinah Glory of the Lord. All Israel encamped around that glory. God was in their midst, but his glory he hid within the Ark of the Covenant, which stood behind the thick linen veil that separated the public room of the Tabernacle from the Holy of Holies deep within it.

Israel practically made a fetish of the ark. During the dark days of the sons of Eli the high priest, the priesthood had sunk so low that God brought judgment upon the house of Eli.

The Philistines defeated Israel and took the Ark of the Covenant to Ashdod; took it into the house of Dagon, their pagan fish god, and set it beside the idol of Dagon. The next morning the Philistines found the idol of Dagon had fallen face forward to the ground. They set the idol back in its place. Entering the house of Dagon the next day they found the idol on the ground again, but this time its head and hands were on the floor separated from the fish-like body. The presence of the Lord with the ark had caused the pagan idol to crash to the ground.

In addition, the Lord smote the Philistines with painful tumors or hemorrhoids. The people in Ashdod felt they had to get rid of the powerful God of the Hebrews, so they sent the ark to Gath and then to Ekron with the same tragic results in each city. For the seven months the Philistines kept the ark in their possession, they suffered under the judgment of God.

Determined to get rid of the ark, the Philistines placed it on a new cart hitched to two cows and sent it back to Israel along with an offering of five golden tumors and five golden mice, which they placed beside the ark. With no driver the cows pulled the cart and the ark to a place called Bethshemesh.

Study the Sin of the Bethshemites

The people of Bethshemesh so rejoiced to see the ark that they broke up the cart and offered the two cows as a burnt offering unto the Lord. Then the people committed a great sin. They looked inside the ark. God considered their sin to be so offensive to him that he slew 50,070 inhabitants of Bethshemesh (1 Samuel 6:19).

To put that number in perspective, it was more than both the Confederate and Union armies lost at Gettysburg—the bloodiest battle of the Civil War! Why did God cause such a slaughter? Because he is holy and the Bethshemites had violated his clear instruction for handling the ark of the Lord. They, who were sinners, had attempted to approach the Lord who, because of his holiness, was unapproachable to them.

When David ascended the throne of Israel, unlike Saul, his predecessor, he acknowledged that he could not rule the nation without the presence, power, and glory of God. He captured the stronghold of Zion, renaming it "The City of David" and proceeded under God's blessing to defeat the Philistines. Then he gathered 30,000 men to fetch the ark from the house of Abinadab, where it had been for twenty years out of its place in the tabernacle at Gibeon.

Know Why God Judged Uzzah

David placed the ark on a new cart and commanded Ahio and Uzzah, the sons of Abinadab, to drive the oxen pulling the cart. David and the people of Israel played all manner of instruments before the Lord. For twenty years the Presence had dwelt in the home of Abinadab to his blessing and preservation. It had been away from the tabernacle, its appointments, sacrifices, and functioning priesthood. In utter contrast to what was shortly to take place, David and the people stood in the awesome, unhidden Presence—playing and singing praises to God's glory and lived!

When the oxen pulling the cart stumbled, Uzzah, one of the drivers, was afraid that the ark would fall off the cart. So he put out his hand to steady it. Again, this was a great sin because it violated God's instructions for handling the ark. Consequently, God's anger was kindled against Uzzah and God smote him dead.

The incident struck fear into David. Afraid of the Lord, he would not take the ark into the City of David. Instead he had the men carry it aside into the house of Obededom, where it remained for three months. The Bible says that, as a consequence, the Lord blessed Obededom and his household.

When David heard that the Lord had blessed Obededom because of the presence of the ark he had the ark brought to the City of David with great joy and gladness. They had carried it only six paces when David sacrificed oxen and fatlings to the Lord and danced before him with all his might. In obedience to the Lord's instructions, David used the Levites to carry the ark to its proper place because he knew why the Lord had judged Uzzah and the Bethshemites. They had violated God's commandment concerning the ark, to treat it as holy.

As the ark was brought to Zion and placed in the midst of the tent David had pitched for it near his own house, his and the people's joy knew no bounds. It was away from the tabernacle in Gibeon with its divine services. Amazingly, David performed the prescribed duties of the priesthood and lived! He offered burnt sacrifices and peace offerings before God and appointed certain of the Levites to minister openly before the ark of the Lord and to record and praise the Lord God of Israel.

Others also openly and continually ministered before the ark with musical instruments. All this was done away from the curtains, the veils, the darkness, and the prior forbidden entrance into the Holiness of his presence on pain of death. Yet now, all is glory unhidden, unveiled, open in his presence! God mightily blessed the people as they worshiped him. There was no fear of judgment as the people rejoiced in his blessed unveiled presence and lived. This, I think, is what the Bible means by the Tabernacle of David.

Examine the Scofield Bible Notes

It seems to me that *The Scofield Reference Bible* commentary on 1 Chronicles 16:37 misses the true meaning of the Tabernacle of David. In his notes on page 475, Scofield wrote, "It will be understood that the ancient tabernacle was now divided; the ark was brought into 'Zion' while the brazen altar, at least, and probably the vessels of the holy place, were established in the high place at Gibeon."

"Asaph and the singers were 'left before the ark' while the priests ministered in Gibeon before the tabernacle. All this was mere confusion. With the construction of the temple the divine order seems to be restored" (p. 475).

I don't see how this exposition can be true because God blessed the household of Abinadab for twenty years while the ark was in his home. He also blessed the household of Obededom for three months when the ark was in his home. In addition the Lord blessed David for forty years while the ark was located in Zion.

Scofield must be in error when he says, "All this was mere confusion." The Bible says that "God is not the author of confusion" (1 Corinthians 14:33). Since this is true, he certainly would not bless confusion for more than half a century.

Learn the Prophecies About David's Tabernacle

"And thine house and thy kingdom shall be established forever before thee: thy throne shall be established for ever" (1 Samuel 7:16). This all-encompassing prophecy was made by the Lord through Nathan the prophet to David the king of Israel.

David's son Solomon would build the house or temple of the Lord that the Lord did not permit David to build. David's greater son, however, the *Branch,* or Jesus Christ, would build the true house and temple of the Lord (Zechariah 6:12–15).

Solomon built the physical temple on Mount Moriah (1 Chronicles 3:1), but the true temple would encompass Zion (Psalm 132:13–18). The "Zion" intended here was not a hill in Jerusalem. For its foundation, see Isaiah 52, 59, 60, and, in particular, Isaiah 28:16: "Therefore thus saith the Lord GOD, Behold, I lay in Zion for a foundation of stone, a tried stone, a precious cornerstone, a sure foundation: he that believeth shall not make haste."

Writing in the New Testament, Peter referred to this prophecy when he wrote, "Wherefore also it is contained in the scripture. Behold, I lay in Zion a chief cornerstone, elect, precious: and he that believeth on him shall not be confounded. Unto you therefore which believe he is precious: but unto them which be disobedient, the stone which the builders disallowed, the same is made the head of the corner" (1 Peter 2:6–7).

In order to obtain a correct interpretation of all this we must keep in mind that the historical tabernacle of David was the little tent he pitched on his own property in which he placed the ark of the Lord. It was there that David met with the Lord, communed with him, openly worshiped and praised him, and appointed Levites to minister before him.

David did all of this away from the tabernacle in Gibeon with its divinely ordained services and a priesthood that ministered before a veiled and hidden Presence. As we have seen, the slightest deviation from that divine order brought instant judgment. Yet God in David's tabernacle, that is the tent, blessed and guided him for his entire forty-year reign.

Know Why God Favored David

The question arises, "Why did God punish the Bethshemites for looking in the ark, Uzzah for placing his hand on the ark, and the sons of Aaron for burning strange fire in the tabernacle (Leviticus 10:1–3), but blessed David for having the ark in a tent on his own property?

Apparently the Lord gives some of his special servants privileges and insights that he does not give to others. For example, Jesus said, "Your father Abraham rejoiced to see my day: and he saw it and was glad" (John 8:36). The Bible says, "And the Lord spake unto Moses face to face, as a man speaketh unto his friend" (Exodus 33:11). This caused his face to shine so that he had to wear a veil when speaking to the people of Israel (Exodus 34:33 and 2 Corinthians 3:13).

Moses was different from all other prophets. The Lord said that while he spoke to other prophets in dreams and visions it was not so with Moses, "who is faithful in all my house. With him will I speak mouth to mouth, even apparently, and not in dark speeches; and the similitude of the Lord shall he behold" (Numbers 12:6–8). Job, Noah, Daniel, Peter, and Paul also received special favors and recognition from the Lord.

Only about David, however, do we read these words from the Lord: "I have found David the son of Jesse, a man after mine own heart, which shall fulfill all my will" (Acts 13:22). Most people know only that David killed Goliath, was king of Israel, committed adultery with Bathsheba, the wife of Uriah, and wrote some of the Psalms. But the Bible says that David had a special relationship with God that few men experience. Could it be that God wanted to give David a taste of what millions of Christians experience? They and he communed with God without the ceremonial requirements of the tabernacle and temple.

Psalm 89 shows the exaltation of David and the high position in which God placed him. It speaks both of David and the Lord Jesus Christ, who was called the Son of David. The tabernacle of David seems to be God's reward to David for his faithfulness and devotion to him in spite of a life laced with hardships and sorrow.

Read What Noted Expositors Say

Once we come to understand the spiritual meaning of the tabernacle of David, we are saddened to know that many of God's children have been deceived by the teaching in the notes of *The Scofield Reference Bible*. It is also sad that most Christians believe erroneous prophetic speculations and the faulty exegesis being taught today. How much better off they would be to study what the great expositors of the past have written about some of the difficult portions of the Bible! Here, for example, are comments from three of them which bolster this chapter's position on David's tabernacle:

> **Jamieson, Fawcet and Brown on Acts 15:14–17:** The point of the passage lies in the predicted purpose of God, under the new economy that the "heathen" or "Gentiles" should be called by his name or have his name called upon them. By the building again of the fallen tabernacle of David or restoring its decayed splendor, is meant that only and more glorious recovery which it was to experience under David's Son and Lord.

> **G. Campbell Morgan on Acts 15:16–17:** A prophecy fulfilled in principle on the day of Pentecost when that little Hebrew community became the true Israel of God; and immediately following, when the prophetic promise was fulfilled in the experience of the Gentiles.[1]

> **Matthew Henry on Amos 9:11–12:** The church militant, in its present state, dwelling in shepherds' tents to feed, as in soldiers' tents to fight, is the tabernacle of David. David's kingdom was restored in Christ the Messiah.[2]

---

1. G. Campbell Morgan, G.L., *The Acts of the Apostles* (Fleming H. Revell Company), 362.

2. Matthew Henry, *Commentary on the Whole Bible* (Grand Rapids, Michigan: Zondervan Publishing House), 1137.

Matthew Henry on Acts 15:16–17: Most of the Old Testament prophets spoke more or less of the calling in of the Gentiles. It was the general expectation of the pious Jews that the Messiah should be a light to enlighten the Gentiles (Luke 2:32); but James waives the more illustrious prophecies of this, and pitches upon one that seemed more obscure: Amos 9:11–12 where it is foretold: (1) the setting up of the kingdom of the Messiah (verse 16), "I will raise up the tabernacle of David that is fallen down." The tabernacle was ruined and fallen down; there had not been for many ages a king of the house of David. But God will return, and will build it again, raise it out of its ruins, a phoenix out of its ashes; and this was now lately fulfilled, when our Lord Jesus was raised out of that family. The church of Christ may be called the tabernacle of David. This may sometimes be brought very low, and may seem to be in ruins, but it shall be built again, its withering interests shall revive. (2) The bringing in of the Gentiles as the effect and consequence of this (v. 17) . . . the uniting of Jews and Gentiles in one body, and all those things that were done in order to do it were what God did.[3]

The Bible says that the throne and tabernacle of David are identical. "And in mercy shall the throne be established: and he shall sit upon it in truth in the tabernacle of David, judging and seeking judgment and hasting righteousness" (Isaiah 16:5).

Since the raising up of the tabernacle of David has been proven to have taken place in this dispensation, why look for it to happen in a future dispensation? What biblical warrant is there to anticipate the fulfillment of these predictions some two thousand years or more after they were made? In Acts 2:29–32, Peter gave the right interpretation to his audience on the day of Pentecost in the first century A.D. when he said:

Men and brethren, let me freely speak unto you of the patriarch David, that he is both dead and buried, and his sepulcher is with

---

3. Ibid, p. 1695.

us unto this day. Therefore being a prophet, and knowing that God had sworn with an oath to him, that of the fruit of his loins, according to the flesh, he would raise up Christ to sit on his throne; He seeing this before spake of the resurrection of Christ, that his soul was not left in hell, neither his flesh did see corruption. This Jesus hath God raised up, whereof we all are witnesses.

Understand Your Position in Christ

Like David in his tabernacle of old, we through the blood of the Everlasting Covenant are always in the presence of God because the veil of the temple has been rent from top to bottom. Now, in Christ Jesus, heaven's one High Priest, we stand in the holiest on the basis of his once-for-all sacrifice for our sins. As believer priests, we offer up spiritual sacrifices to our God. By singing psalms, hymns, and spiritual songs, we commune with him through the Shekinah Glory of the Holy Spirit now dwelling within us.

"For ye are the temple of the living God," said Paul; "as God hath said, I will dwell in them, and walk in them; and I will be their God, and they shall be my people." (2 Corinthians 6:16)

Though many Christians have failed to grasp an understanding of this position we have in Christ, the Bible, writing to Christians, says, "But ye are come to Mount Zion, and unto the city of the living God, the heavenly Jerusalem" (Hebrews 12:22). It does not say "will come," but "are come" to Mount Zion.

As a Christian, you are already there; you have arrived! Abraham and his descendants looked for a city which has foundations, whose builder and maker is God. They sought a better country, that is, an heavenly country (Hebrews 11:10, 14, 16). But you and I have come to that heavenly country which they sought! Paul the Apostle explained all of this, and our position in Christ, with these beautiful words from his Epistle to the Ephesians:

But God, *who* is rich in mercy, for his great love wherewith he loved us, even when we were dead in sins, hath quickened us together with Christ, (by grace ye are saved;) And hath raised us up together, and made us sit together in heavenly places in Christ Jesus: That in the ages to come he might shew the exceeding riches of his grace in his kindness toward us through Christ Jesus. (Ephesians 2:4–7)

I trust that God has used these suggestions to help you solve the mystery of the tabernacle of David and given you an increased understanding of your place in the spiritual Zion and your position in Christ *right now*. Here are a few lines from the hymn by Benjamin Schmolck that should help us all to increase our appreciation of Zion—the church of Jesus Christ:

> Open now thy gates of beauty,
> Zion, let me enter there,
> Where my soul in joyful duty
> Waits for him who answers prayer.
> Oh how blessed is this place,
> Filled with solace, light and grace!
>
> Speak, O God, and I will hear thee,
> Let thy will be done indeed;
> May I undisturbed draw near thee
> While thou dost thy people feed.
> Here of life the fountain flows,
> Here is balm for all our woes.

CHAPTER ELEVEN

Does It Really Matter?

The Jordan River is not as beautiful as some rivers. It is rapid, sometimes turbulent, and in some places deep and treacherous. Naaman, the leprous Syrian general, complained when Elisha told him he could be healed by dipping himself seven times in the waters of Jordan. "Are not Abana and Pharpar, rivers of Damascus," he argued, "better than all the waters of Israel?" (2 Kings 5:12). Yet after doing what he was told to do he was healed.

About six hundred years later, in the first century A.D., another event took place at the River Jordan. It was unique in that nothing like it had ever taken place before and it could never be repeated. It was the baptism of Jesus Christ, the Son of God! Standing waist deep in the Jordan River stood John the Baptist in his coat of camel's hair. By his side stood Christ, the Son of God. And on the bank stood a multitude of people who had come to hear John preach.

They watched as John baptized Christ and lifted him up out of the water. As he rose out of the water, Jesus saw the heavens opening and the Holy Spirit, like a dove, descending upon him. Then a voice came from heaven saying, "Thou art my beloved Son in whom I am well pleased" (Mark 1:10–11).

God must have considered this occasion to be of great significance because it is the only event in the scriptural record when the triune

God manifested himself in his three persons—Father, Son, and Holy Spirit—at the same time!

Men and women are not to perceive the manifestations and commandments of the Lord as trivial. Some skip over the Lord's personal instructions to Moses in the book of Exodus about how the tabernacle was to be built because of the many details it includes. What if Moses had considered the details too trivial to bother with and had disobeyed God's command to build the tabernacle according to the pattern that had been given to him on Mount Sinai? Such conduct would have produced two tragedies: first, Moses would have been guilty of disobeying God; and second, the divine pattern for building the tabernacle would have been destroyed.

Ever since Adam and Eve sinned in the Garden of Eden, man has made the mistake of not thinking consequentially. Thus, mankind is still suffering from the consequences of the sins committed by his first parents. In another example, Achan's sin of stealing gold and silver and a costly garment from the city of Jericho brought about the death of thirty-six of his fellow Israelites and the nation of Israel being shamefully beaten in the Battle of Ai (Joshua 7:1–26).

Moses was kept out of the land of promise because instead of *speaking* to the rock to get water for the children of Israel (as God had commanded him to do), he struck it. Moses' greatest desire was to lead the people into the land of Canaan. As he stood on Mount Nebo, looking over the Promised Land, how disappointing it must have been for him to hear the Lord's refusal to let him go over Jordan! "I have caused thee to see it with thine eyes," said the Lord, "but thou shalt not go over thither!" (Deuteronomy 34:4).

Some go through life thinking that God has changed and no longer punishes disobedience, but, according to the Bible, he never changes. "I am the Lord," he said, "I change not" (Malachi 3:6). And the Bible describes Jesus Christ, the second person of the divine trinity, as "the same yesterday, and today, and forever" (Hebrews 13:8).

This *immutability* of God poses questions about baptism, an ordinance of the church commanded by Christ: Are churches free to change what the Bible teaches about baptism? For example, do churches have the authority to change the time in a person's life when he or she is to be baptized? Do they have the right to change the biblical candidates for baptism?

Do churches have any biblical authority for changing the mode of baptism from that mode clearly given in God's Word? And last, but not least, do men and women have any warrant for saying baptism is not important? Baptism is an *unusual topic* because of the confusion caused by the differing views about it. If you have a sincere desire to know the truth about Christian baptism, read this chapter with an open mind, as together we examine five facts: 1) Churches Acknowledge the Truth about Baptism; 2) Churches Admit to a Mistranslation of Baptism: 3) Churches Disobey the Lord Concerning Baptism; 4) Some Say That Baptism Is Not Important; and, 5) Baptism Caused Me to Leave Presbyterianism.

Churches Acknowledge the Truth about Baptism

One of the most amazing facts in the history of Christianity is the variety of changes to the simple ordinance of Christian baptism made by churchmen, many of whom acknowledged the truth about baptism. Most of those churches who have made the changes agree that, for the first three hundred years of Christian practice, believers only were baptized and that by immersion.

In his book *Christian Baptism*, the late John Murray, who believed in infant baptism, said that there is no objection to this proposition: "There is no express command to baptize infants and no record in the New Testament of a clear case of infant baptism." He then tried to explain the difference between his position and the Bible's by saying, "What can be deduced from Scripture is of authority in the church of God as well as what is expressly set down in Scripture" (p. 69).

It would be impossible, however, to deduce the idea of infant baptism from the divinely inspired New Testament because there is not even one hint of such a practice. The New Testament also does not record one incident of a baptism by sprinkling or pouring. Many of the founders of church denominations that changed the ordinance agreed that this is true. For example, John Wesley, founder of the Methodist Church, said that the phrase "buried by baptism" in Romans 6:4, "refers to the ancient mode of baptism which was by immersion."

In Book IV of his *Institutes of the Christian Religion* John Calvin, the Founder of the Reformed and Presbyterian churches, wrote, "It is evident that the term baptism means to immerse." In his commentary on the baptism of the Ethiopian eunuch in Acts 8, Calvin also wrote, "Here we see how baptism was administered among the ancients; for they immersed the whole body in water."

Marcus Dods, a leading New Testament scholar of the Presbyterians in Scotland, said, "Man is dead and buried in the water, and he rises from his cleansing grave a new man. The full significance of the rite would have been lost had immersion not been practiced."

Alfred Plummer, a famous scholar of the Church of England, said, "A death to sin was expressed by the plunge beneath the water, and rising again to a life of righteousness by the return of light and air; and hence the appropriateness of immersion."

Immersion was also taught by A. T. Robertson, a world-renowned scholar in the Greek language. "Every passage in the New Testament," he said, "is intelligible with the meaning of immersion. No instance has ever been found in any Greek writing where *baptizo* (the Greek word from whence is derived the English word baptism) means to sprinkle or to pour. It always means to dip either literally or metaphorically. The New Testament uses *rantizo* for sprinkle and *eccheo* for pour, but neither of these occurs in the New Testament for the act of baptism, but always *baptizo* is used, which means to dip or immerse."

The most enlightening words I ever read on baptism were written by J. N. Frost. "Pouring or sprinkling," he said, "tells what is done with water. Baptism or immersion tells what is done with *the person*. You may sprinkle water, you may pour water, but you do not baptize water! You baptize or immerse *the person*. When our Lord commanded us to make disciples and baptize or immerse them, he did not say sprinkle water on them, he said *baptize them.*"

One of the outstanding proofs that immersion is the correct way to baptize is the rite of baptism in the Greek Orthodox Church. If anyone should know what the Greek word *baptizo* means it should be a Greek. Ministers of the Greek Church practice infant baptism, but they immerse the infant because *baptizo* means "immerse."

Churches Admit to a Mistranslation of *Baptism*

Why do the English Bibles use "baptize" when the Greek word *baptizo* means immerse? The answer is twofold: fear and disobedience. The fifty-four outstanding scholars who translated the Authorized King James Version of the Bible in 1611 knew that the word *baptizo* in the Greek New Testament meant immersion. They dared not translate it immerse, however, because the Church of England sprinkled children and adults.

When they conferred with King James I, who was head of the Church of England, he requested that they Anglicize *baptizo* rather than translate it. Consequently the English Bible has the anglicized Greek word "baptize" instead of "immerse"—the correct English translation.

Once the error was introduced to the church, it spread. On July 1, 1833, the British and Foreign Bible Society of England, composed of evangelical denominations, passed a resolution in which they declined aid to translators of the Bible in foreign languages, unless "the Greek terms relating to baptism be rendered, either according to the principles adopted by the translators of the authorized version, by a word derived from the original, or by such terms as may be considered unobjectionable by the other denominations of Christians composing the Bible Society."

Churches and translators admitted to "disobedience, not only in translation, but in the practice of baptism. The Roman Catholic Church later admitted they had changed the ordinance of baptism in the Fourth Century A.D. because sprinkling was more convenient. Here is a direct quotation from the Roman Catholic book, *Faith of Our Fathers*:

> For several centuries after the establishment of Christianity baptism was conferred by immersion. But since the Twelfth Century baptism by sprinkling has prevailed in the Catholic Church. Baptism is the essential means established for washing away the stain of original sin, and the door by which we find admittance into the church. Hence baptism is as essential for the infant as for the full-grown man. Unbaptized infants are excluded from the kingdom of heaven. Baptism makes us heirs of heaven and coheirs with Jesus Christ. (pp. 316–317)

Instead of fighting or objecting to this heresy, the Protestant Reformers went along with it. John Calvin said, "Whether the person baptized is to be wholly immersed, or whether he is only to be sprinkled with water is not of the least consequence: the churches should be at liberty to adopt either according to the diversity of the climate, although it is evident that the term baptize means *to immerse.*"

It is difficult to understand how one of the greatest expositors and theologians of the Reformation could be so blinded as to make such a statement of error with regard to the mode of baptism! In effect he said: The mode did not matter; churches could use whatever mode they chose; and climate was a criterion by which to judge how to administer this important ordinance commanded by the Lord Jesus Christ!

The translation from Greek to English is of the utmost importance when it comes to translating the New Testament. To make deliberate mistranslations of the Greek words has dire consequences. For instance, from the time of the Protestant Reformers to the present hour those who know what the Bible teaches believe the Roman Catholic Church was wrong to translate *metanoeo,* the Greek word for "repent" or "change your mind" to "do penance" in its Douay Version of the Bible. That one wrong translation changed the message of the whole process of salvation from salvation by grace alone to salvation by works.

Protestants made a similar error when they transliterated *baptizo* into "baptize" instead of using "immerse" the proper English translation. That one deliberate mistranslation in the Authorized King James Bible has had far reaching consequences of a most tragic nature.

For example, the Bible societies of England and America will not let missionaries correctly translate *baptizo* into a foreign language. For nearly four hundred years millions of Christians were led to believe the lie that infant sprinkling, which the apostles never taught or practiced, was a Christian baptism. Some even think that their children must be sprinkled to be sure of heaven!

Churches Disobey the Lord Concerning Baptism

"Are Roman Catholic baptisms and ordinations valid?" This was the question presented for a decision by the 1854 Presbyterian General Assembly of America in the city of Buffalo. After a heated discussion, the majority report said that all ordinations at the hands of Roman Catholic priests were invalid, because the Roman Catholic Church was no true church of Jesus Christ, but antichrist on many practices and doctrines, and therefore the baptisms and ordinations of such an apostate body were null and void.

The minority report, however, contended that if they denied the Church of Rome to be a true church of Christ, they unchurched themselves, since they came out of Rome and received their baptism and ordinations therefrom. Finding they could not extricate themselves from the dilemma, they moved an indefinite postponement of the question, and that is the way it stands today.

Baptists and other Bible-believing churches that practice baptism by immersion, however, have never been faced with that question because they never came out of Romanism or of any Protestant body. We have learned so far that immersion is the biblically correct mode of baptism.

A church, however, may be right in its *mode* of baptism, yet wrong on the doctrine of baptism. For example, the Greek Orthodox Church baptizes by immersion but it erroneously baptizes infants and teaches the false doctrine of baptismal regeneration—that one is born again by baptism.

The Church of Christ also believes in baptism by immersion but teaches the false doctrine of baptismal regeneration. In his book on *Christian Baptism,* Alexander Campbell, one of the four founders of the church, wrote, "Remission of sins cannot be enjoyed by any person before immersion. Belief of this testimony is what impelled us into the water, knowing that the efficacy of his [Christ's] Blood is to be communicated to our conscience in the way God has pleased to appoint: we stagger not at the promise to flee to the sacred ordinance which brought the Blood of Jesus in contact with our consciences. Without knowing and believing this, immersion is a blasted nut, the shell is there but the kernel is wanting" (p. 521).

The Bible puts the Blood of Christ before the water of baptism and teaches, not that baptism is essential to salvation, but that salvation is essential to baptism. Some denominations teach that one must go through the waters of baptism to receive salvation by the shed Blood of Christ. But the Bible teaches that one must go through the Blood to receive the waters of baptism.

Campbell also said, "I am bold to affirm that everyone who in belief of what the apostles spoke was immersed, did, in the very instant in which he or she was put under water, receive the forgiveness of sins and the gift of the Holy Spirit."

The Bible, however, contains no such teaching. In the presence of Gentiles who had just been converted to Christ, Peter the apostle said this: "Can any man forbid water, that these should not be baptized, who have received the Holy Spirit as well as we?" (Acts 10:47).

It is obvious that for the apostles the order was reception of the Holy Spirit and *then* baptism by immersion. Those churches who think that the baptism of sinners makes them Christians are wrong, because the Bible teaches that the church is to baptize those who are already Christians.

Baptismal regeneration is even worse than infant baptism because those church officials who teach that one is born again by baptism baptize adults. That is why Bible believing churches call biblical baptism by immersion *believer's baptism.*

The most popular sermon of the thousands preached and published by Charles Spurgeon was the one on *Baptismal Regeneration.* In it, he exposed and refuted the false doctrine of baptism taught and practiced by the Church of England.

Some Say That Baptism Is Not Important

Some argue that baptism is not important and that the mode of baptism is likewise not important. The unique event of Christ's baptism, however, proves them to be wrong. Christ thought his baptism was so important that he walked sixty miles from Nazareth to the place on the Jordan where John was baptizing.

Another thing that proves baptism is very important to the Lord is this: After his Resurrection and prior to his Ascension to heaven, Jesus commanded his apostles to make disciples of people in all nations "baptizing them in the name of the Father, and of the Son, and of the Holy Ghost: teaching them to observe all things whatsoever I have commanded you: and, lo, I am with you alway, even unto the end of the world [or age]" (Matthew 28:19–20).

Those who do not recognize the importance of baptism usually argue against it by saying something like this: "Baptism has nothing to do with salvation and, since it causes division in the church, why not dismiss it altogether?"

It is true that baptism does not save the sinner. It is also true, however, that Jesus Christ commanded his apostles to baptize believers because God uses baptism by immersion to present the divine truth of the Gospel of Christ in symbolic form. It identifies the believer with the death, burial, and resurrection of Jesus Christ. Baptism by immersion is a public confession of one's personal faith in Jesus Christ as Lord and Saviour, his death to sin, and his own resurrection to newness of life.

Millions of people believe that one confesses Christ by responding to an invitation from an evangelist to make a decision, raise his hand, and go forward to where the speaker is waiting to shake his hand. It usually comes as a shock to many Christians when they learn that such an "evangelistic" procedure is not mentioned anywhere in the New Testament.

According to the apostles, baptism was the way to confess one's faith in Jesus Christ. That is still true today. From what one reads in the New Testament, one would conclude that an evangelist who does not baptize those who show evidence of repentance and faith is not obeying Christ's great commission that includes his command to baptize believers.

Paul instructed Christians to keep the ordinances of baptism and the Lord's Table (1 Corinthians 11:2). It is important for us to notice that Paul did not say "change" the ordinances, but "keep" them. Both the ordinances of baptism and the Lord's Table proclaim in symbolic form the death of Jesus Christ for the sins of his people. They are used, in other words, to proclaim the Gospel, which Paul summarized in these words:

> Moreover, brethren, I declare unto you the Gospel *which* I preached unto you, *which,* also ye have received, and wherein ye stand; by which also ye are saved, if ye keep in memory what I preached unto you, unless ye have believed in vain. For I delivered unto you first of all that which I also received, how that Christ died for our sins according to the scriptures; and that he was buried, and that he rose again the third day according to the scriptures. (1 Corinthians 15:1–4)

The Gospel symbol in baptism is lost if the church uses any other mode of baptism than believer's baptism by immersion. Speaking about baptism, Paul used the word "buried" in his Epistles to the Romans and Colossians. Baptism by immersion is the only baptism that presents an accurate symbol of being buried in Christ and dead to sin.

In Romans 1–5, Paul declared that all men are sinners and fall short of the glory of God. He also taught that salvation of sinners is by grace alone through faith alone in Christ alone. Paul knew that some people twisted his salvation-by-grace doctrine by saying that Christians should continue in sin so that God's grace might abound. In response Paul said, "God forbid. How shall we that are dead to sin, live any longer therein?" (Romans 6:2).

When sinners receive Jesus Christ as their Lord and Saviour, they die to the dominion of sin. This is the truth signified in believer's baptism by immersion. By going down into the waters of baptism they testify that, through their grace-and-faith union with Christ, they have been buried with him in death. Having died to sin, they are no longer under its condemnation or bondage. Rising from the waters of baptism, they proclaim that they have been raised in Christ to newness of life that gives them spiritual victory. Paul explained this when he wrote Romans 6:3–5:

> Know ye not, that so many of us as were baptized into Jesus Christ were baptized into his death? Therefore we are buried with him by baptism into death: that like as Christ *was* raised up from the dead by the glory of me Father, even so we also should walk in newness of life. For if we have been planted together in the likeness of his death, we shall be also in the likeness of his resurrection.

From the day of Pentecost baptism has served symbolically as an introductory ordinance. It is the new believer's step of obedience and his public identification with Christ's death, burial, and resurrection. Paul took an illustration from the Old Testament to show the meaning of baptism. He said that the Israelites "were all baptized unto Moses in the cloud and in the [Red] sea" (1 Corinthians 10:2).

Having chosen to follow Moses out of Egypt, the Israelites were identified with him when they trusted him to lead them through the Red Sea on dry ground. In like manner, believers become followers of the Lord Jesus the moment they put their trust in him. By their baptism "into Jesus Christ" they openly identify themselves with him as their leader, Lord, and guide.

Paul wrote, "One Lord, one faith, one baptism" (Ephesians 4:5). Church leaders continue to argue over what Paul meant by *one baptism*. Some say, "He meant water baptism," while others say, "He meant baptism by the Spirit." In his commentary on the *Epistle to the Ephesians,* F. F. Bruce, who is not a Baptist, makes these comments about Paul's "one baptism":

> Baptism in water continued to be the outward visible sign by which individuals *who* believed the Gospel . . . were publicly incorporated into this spirit-baptized fellowship—as we are told in Galatians and Romans—"baptized into Christ." (Galatians 3:27; Romans 6:3) It must be remembered that in New Testament times repentance and faith, regeneration and conversion, baptism in water, reception of the Holy Spirit . . . admission to church fellowship . . . were all part of a complex of events *which* took place in a short time . . . Logically they were distinguishable, but in practice they were all bound up with the transition from the old life to the new. (p. 70)

Baptism, then, is a testimony of our death to sin, of our severance from its domination, and our pledge to live a new life through our grace-and-faith union with Jesus Christ. During the First Century, baptism quickly followed a confession of faith in Christ for salvation and was closely associated with membership in the local church.

History provides a classic example, however, of how the ordinance of baptism was perverted as early as the Fourth Century. Constantine, the Roman Emperor at the time, made Christianity the official state religion of the Roman Empire. When it came to baptism, however, he postponed his own baptism until he was on his deathbed. Why? Because he had been taught and hoped that his baptism would wash away all sins just before he died!

Baptism Caused Me to Leave Presbyterianism

I was brought up in a Presbyterian church, sprinkled with water for church membership when I was twelve years old. I attended a Presbyterian college and was examined and recommended by a Presbyterian synod to a Presbyterian seminary. When some learned of my Presbyterian background they asked, "Why did you become a Baptist minister?"

My shortest and most logical answer was this: "I never found one passage in the Bible that recorded baptism by sprinkling. Neither did I find one incident of baptism prior to a confession of faith in Christ."

Other reasons and facts also led me to seek ordination in the Baptist instead of the Presbyterian Church ministry. In my senior year in the Pittsburgh-Xenia Seminary, the school was united for summer school to the Pittsburgh Seminary of the Presbyterian Church. World War II was being fought and the students were being hurried through for graduation in September so we could leave for the chaplaincy.

Along with thirty to forty others studying for the Presbyterian ministry, I took a course that summer under Dr. Slossar, one of the Pittsburgh Seminary professors. He was not only a highly educated Presbyterian professor, but also a well-known archaeologist. Near the end of his course, he said this:

"Gentlemen, never try to argue the mode of sprinkling for baptism as having any biblical or historical beginning or value. I have excavated churches of the first and second century which had baptisteries almost as large as the church auditorium or meeting place for worship." That day I decided I would never sprinkle babies. Nor would I use that incorrect mode of baptism on adults, having learned that the apostles and early Christians baptized believers by immersion.

Years later my wife verified the professor's words when she traveled to the Holy Land with my mother. She saw the excavated First and Second Century church buildings with huge baptisteries that proved beyond any shade of doubt that the early churches baptized by immersion. Hymnwriter W. W. Sidey caught the biblical meaning of believer's baptism by immersion when he wrote these lines:

Buried with Christ! Our glad hearts say,
Come see the place where once he lay.
Risen with him! Allured by love,
Henceforth we seek the things above.
Walking with him! A life how blest,
Strengthened with might, girt round with rest!
In him abiding! Living vine,
We too would bear the fruit divine.
For him enduring! Pain and loss
Are but the shadow of his Cross.
By him victorious! Smile or frown,
We march right onward to a crown.

CHAPTER TWELVE

The Hounds of Heaven

There is a similarity between the persistence of a hound dog after its prey and the consistent providence of God throughout the life of a believer in Jesus Christ. I have had the privilege of watching hound dogs at work. It didn't matter whether the dog was a rabbit hound, coon hound, fox hound, bear hound, or even a cougar hound—they all had one thing in common: Once they got the scent of a prey, they would put their nose to the trail and, with much barking, would follow that scent no matter where it took them.

I have watched a beagle (rabbit hound) run up both sides of a creek when a rabbit had crossed it in an attempt to throw the hound off its trail. The beagle will come back to where he lost the scent and then try both sides of the creek until he finds the scent where the rabbit left the water. Then he will follow its trail until he finds the rabbit. Hound dogs are, to say the least, persistent!

The Faithful Hounds

The last verse of the most memorized chapter in the Bible contains a reference to God's providence and to what some have called "The Hounds of Heaven." That verse reads, "Surely goodness and mercy shall follow me all the days of my life: and I will dwell in the house of the Lord forever" (Psalm 23:6). Those hounds are the goodness and mercy of God and they never leave off following us for our entire lives. Sinclair Ferguson says, "He sends them to us from his throne of grace; sometimes to bark at us, to badger us; sometimes to woo us by persuading us that his will is good and perfect for our lives."

Most people understand what "goodness" means. Mercy, however, is a different matter. Since there is much misunderstanding of the biblical meaning of mercy, it qualifies for appearance in a book on *unusual topics*. Also because of that misunderstanding, this chapter will concentrate on that wonderful character trait of the Hound of Heaven, the mercy of God.

The Saving Mercy of God

Mercy has many applications, but its most important work has to do with the Lord saving us from our sins and from the punishment we deserved. According to Paul, it was "not by works of righteousness which we have done, but according to his [God's] mercy he saved us, by the washing of regeneration, and renewing of the Holy Ghost" (Titus 3:5).

As Dr. Claude Duval Cole says, "The showing of mercy is the very opposite of leaving sinners to act out their own sinful natures. It is the putting of something good in them, a holy disposition and a good principle, by which they repent of their sins and believe in Christ."[1]

Paul described that redemptive process by saying that "we were by nature the children of wrath, even as others. But God, who is rich in mercy, for his great love wherewith he loved us, even when we were dead in sins, hath made us alive together with Christ (by grace ye are saved)" (Ephesians 2:3–5).

---

1. Claude Duval Cole, *Definitions of Doctrines* 1 (Mortons Gap, Kentucky: First Baptist Church, 1944), 97.

Dr. Cole further says, "It was in mercy that Christ died for us, and it was also in mercy that the Spirit enlightened our sin-darkened understanding. Mercy reminds us of our miserable condition as children of wrath because apart from God's mercy we would be consumed by the wrath of God's justice. Mercy also explains our salvation."[2]

God's Mercy Defined

Webster's Dictionary defines the word "mercy" as "the compassionate treatment of an enemy." In his *Systematic Theology,* Baptist theologian August H. Strong said, "Mercy is the eternal principle of God's nature which leads him to seek the temporal good and eternal salvation of those who have opposed themselves to his will, even at the cost of infinite self-sacrifice."[3]

Robert Haldane, author of a commentary on Romans, said, "Mercy is that adorable perfection in God by which he pities and relieves the miserable." Dr. Cole explains it further:

> Mercy implies that the sinner has nothing to say in his own defense. We understand the meaning of mercy when the defendant throws himself on the mercy of the court. That means that he is guilty and has nothing of merit to plead before the law. And this is exactly the condition of every man of us before the bar of divine justice. Mercy is their only hope. We may plead before our fellow man, but to ask God for justice (to ask God to give us what we deserve) is the same as asking for a room in the regions of the damned.[4]

In the days when Napoleon was the first consul of France, a well-dressed girl of fourteen presented herself alone at the gate of the palace. With her tears and entreaties she moved the kind-hearted

---

2. Claude Duval Cole, *Definitions of Doctrines* 1 (Mortons Gap, Kentucky: First Baptist Church, 1944), 97–98.

3. August H. Strong, *Systematic Theology* (p. 289).

4. Claude Duval Cole, *Definitions of Doctrines* 1 (Mortons Gap, Kentucky: First Baptist Church, 1944), 98.

porter to allow her to enter. Passing from one room to another, she found her way to the hallway through which Napoleon and his officers were to pass.

When he appeared, she cast herself down at his feet and, in the most piteous and moving manner, and cried, "Pardon, Sir! Pardon for my father!"

"And who is your father?" asked Napoleon. "And who are you?"

"My name is Layolia," she said still crying, "but Sir, my father is doomed to die!"

"Ah, young lady," said Napoleon, "I can do nothing for you. It is the second time in which your father has been found guilty of treason against the state."

"Yes," cried the poor girl, "I know it, Sire, but I do not ask for justice. I implore mercy! I beseech you, forgive, oh *forgive* my father!"

Napoleon's lips trembled, and his eyes filled with tears. After a momentary struggle of feeling, he gently took the hand of the young maiden, and said, "Well, my child, for your sake I will pardon your father. That is enough. Now leave me."

GOD'S MERCY DESCRIBED

God's Mercy Is Great

Among the various descriptions of mercy, the foremost is greatness. King Solomon said that God had shown great mercy to his father David because he had walked before God in truth (1 Kings 3:6). This was a manifestation of God's nature. The Bible says, "For as the heaven is high above the earth, so great is his mercy toward them that fear him" (Psalm 103:11). "The Lord is gracious, and full of compassion; slow to anger, and of great mercy" (145:8).

God's mercy is great because its source is our infinite God, the Father. It is also great because of what it cost God to extend it to us. Our sin had blocked the way and had to be dealt with. To remove that obstacle, Christ had to suffer, shed his Blood, and die as our substitute.

By imputing our guilt to him and causing him to be punished on our behalf, God was able to impute Christ's righteousness to us and to justify us in his sight. But it all began with his great mercy.

His mercy is great, too, because it is plenteous (Psalm 103:8). He does not grudgingly dole out his mercy, but daily showers it upon us.

God's Mercy Is Rich, Tender, Wide, and Abundant

Paul said that God "is rich in mercy" (Ephesians 2:4), but God does not keep the riches of his mercy to himself. Like Joseph, who gave of his abundance to his unworthy brethren, even so the Lord gives us of his fullness. The riches of his redemptive and providential mercy are beyond calculation.

They are impossible to catalogue because, like God himself, the riches of his mercy are infinite. Showered daily upon his people, the riches of his mercy include the whole range of redemptive and providential blessings. Think for a moment of the tremendous riches that are ours at the mercy seat where we kneel in prayer "to obtain mercy and find grace to help in time of need" (Hebrews 4:16).

Though incalculable in riches, the mercy of God is also tender. One of the most touching statements concerning the Incarnation of Jesus was uttered by a man who had been completely dumbstruck for nine months previous: "Through the tender mercy of our God," said Zacharias, father of John the Baptist; "whereby the dayspring from on high hath visited us" (Luke 1:78). It was by the mercy of God that Christ came to earth to live a vicarious life and die a sacrificial death to save his people from their sins.

Every time a person is born again by the Spirit of God it is the result of God's abundant mercy. "Blessed be the God and Father of our Lord Jesus Christ," said Peter, "which according to his abundant mercy hath begotten us again unto a living hope by the resurrection of Jesus Christ from the dead" (1 Peter 1:3). God's mercy is not like a brook that dries up under the heat of summer. It is like a sea without shores—unlimited in its reach to bless. That similitude moved Frederick W. Faber to write these lines:

> There's a wideness in God's mercy,
> Like the wideness of the sea;
> There's a kindness in his justice,
> Which is more than liberty.
> There is welcome for the sinner,
> And more graces for the good;
> There is mercy with the Saviour,
> There is healing in his Blood.

God's Mercy Comes Through Christ

"Redemption," said John Gill, predecessor to Charles Spurgeon, "is a glaring instance of the mercy of God." Though justice had to be satisfied by the doing and dying of Christ, it was divine mercy that sent him to redeem us. In the offering of his life, Christ met all the proscriptive demands of the Law and in his death he met all of the Law's penal demands on our behalf. Here are Dr. Cole's comments:

> Christ did not bring the mercy of God to us. It was the mercy of God that brought Christ to us. Christ is the channel of mercy, not the cause of mercy. The death of Christ makes it possible for God to righteously bestow covenant mercies on his people, justice having been fully satisfied by Christ the Surety. Mercy comes from God, but we have a concrete example of the mercy of God in the regeneration of Saul of Tarsus. He attributes his conversion to the mercy of God. He says that he was once a blasphemer, and a persecutor, and injurious, "but I obtained mercy," says he, "because I did it ignorantly in unbelief" (1 Timothy 1:13). This does not mean that ignorance and unbelief were the ground of mercy, but the evidence that his salvation was an act of mercy. Paul was the

chief of sinners, but he obtained mercy. There is no sinner too bad for mercy to save.[5]

Paul the Apostle confessed to being the chief of sinners, which proves the truth of Christ's comforting statement in Matthew 12:31, where he said, "All manner of sin and blasphemy shall be forgiven unto men." As Cole says, "It is so comforting for us poor sinners to know that God is so rich and abundant in the very thing we so greatly need as sinners. No wonder the psalmist said, "I will sing aloud of thy mercy" (Psalm 59:16).[6]

GOD'S MERCY DISTINGUISHED

Mercy Not Synonymous with Grace

We are safe in saying that most Christians make no distinction between grace and mercy, but perceive them to be synonymous. But the Bible reveals a difference between them, even though there are some things about them that are similar. Dr. Cole explains:

"Mercy and grace have much in common, and yet there are shades of distinction between them. Grace views man without merit; mercy views him as miserable. Grace can be exercised where there is no sin; mercy can be shown only to sinners. The distinction can be seen in the divine dealings with unfallen angels. God has never exercised any mercy toward them, for they have never sinned, and are not, therefore, in a miserable condition. And yet they have been the objects of grace. It was by his grace that God chose them out of the whole angelic race (1 Timothy 5:21). It was in grace that he made Christ their Head (Colossians 2:10; 1 Peter 3:22). And it was in grace that he gave them such honorable commissions. (Hebrews 1:14) God has dealt with the holy angels in grace, for they have not

---

5. Claude Duval Cole, *Definitions of Doctrines* 1 (Mortons Gap, Kentucky: First Baptist Church, 1944), 100.

6. Op cit, p. 98.

merited his favors. If angels cannot merit his favors, what hope is there that sinful men can do so?"[7]

Why Does Mercy Come in After Grace?

Because mercy is the wondrous provision of God to meet the desperate needs of a people who have failed to respond to his grace. We can see this in Exodus 33:19:

> And he said, "I will make all my goodness pass before thee, and I will proclaim the name of the LORD before thee; and will be gracious to whom I will be gracious, and will shew mercy on whom I will shew mercy."

Commenting on this verse, Arthur W. Pink wrote:

> From Egypt to Sinai God had dealt with Israel on the ground of pure grace. In themselves they were no better than the Egyptians, yet God in his sovereignty had brought them out of bondage, conducted them through the Red Sea, separated them unto himself, supplied their every need in the wilderness. But what was their reaction? They had revolted against him, they had repudiated him, they had set up an idol in his place. Could a God whose favors had been so lightly esteemed go on with them any further?

> In the nineteenth verse of Exodus 33 we have one of the most blessed revelations of God's character revealed anywhere in the Bible. Something had been made known here which had never before been revealed in its real depths—his *mercy.*

> It is true this Word was given before in the Book of Genesis, but the full interpretation of its meaning is not discovered until we come to this great declaration that is later incorporated into the Ninth Chapter of Romans. When the divine overflow of God's grace had

---

7. Claude Duval Cole, *Definitions of Doctrines* 1 (Mortons Gap, Kentucky: First Baptist Church, 1944), 98–99.

been abused, his righteous law had been broken, the covenant of Sinai broken by rebellion. Now the only resource left for Israel was the exercise of mercy. When God took up the cause of the slaves in Egypt, there was nothing but grace after grace poured out, but when that was spurned, we now entered a different ground—mercy.[8]

God's Mercy Is Eternal

The word *mercy* is used in the Old Testament like no other word in the Bible. Every one of the twenty-six verses in Psalm 136, for instance, ends with a reference to mercy: "for his mercy endureth for ever." The word, "endureth" is shown in italics, which means it was not in the original Hebrew. So it should read: "His mercy forever."

As a pastor I would often have the congregation read Psalm 136 responsively. I would read the first part of each verse and the people would respond by reading the words "His mercy endureth for ever" twenty-six times. I did this to remind sinners and saints that God's mercy is great, abundant, all-encompassing, eternal, and sovereign.

Most theologians agree that Paul's Epistle to the Romans is the greatest treatise on salvation in print. After writing eleven chapters on doctrine, Paul begins Chapter 12 with this plea: "I beseech you therefore, brethren, by the mercies of God, that ye present your bodies a living sacrifice, wholly acceptable unto God, which is your reasonable service."

Pastors should have mercy in mind when they preach. As Dr. Cole says, "The mercy of God is the proper appeal of the pastor to his people. The pastor is not a man with a big stick; he is God's man with a big Book, and a mighty appeal."[9]

---

8. Arthur W. Pink, *Gleanings in Exodus* (Chicago: Moody Press, 1929), 245.

9. Claude Duval Cole, *Definitions of Doctrines* 1 (Mortons Gap, Kentucky: First Baptist Church, 1944), 101.

God's Mercy Seat

Some Christians, when they read the Bible, make no distinction between what was written for the Israelites and what was written for the church. Take the subject of the mercy seat, for example. It is treated quite differently in the two Testaments. In his exposition of this, Dr. Cole says:

> The mercy seat of the O.T. and the mercy seat of the N.T. are quite distinct, and must not be confused. The one is the type; the other is the antitype. Under the ceremonial law the mercy seat was the lid or covering to the Ark of the Covenant (Hebrews 9:5). This mercy seat was the meeting place between God and Israel. Without this provision of mercy, his presence among them would have been their doom—they would have been consumed by his holy wrath. He could show them mercy and let them live because his justice had found satisfaction in the death of their sin offering—the lamb upon whose head their sins had been confessed and in this way transferred from the sinner to the lamb. The lamb thus made responsible for their sins had to die. Its blood on the mercy sea was the basis of peace between a sinful people and a holy God. Now the blood of bulls and goats could not take away sins except in a typical and ceremonial sense, and then only for a year. Its value was in pointing to a better sacrifice, even the Lamb of God which taketh away the sin of the world. (John 1:29)[10]

The laws of hermeneutics or biblical interpretation include the Christocentric Law, which says that we should "acknowledge that Jesus Christ is the key to interpret, understand, and unify the Scriptures." Another law says, "Always interpret the Old Testament by what you read in the New Testament."

There are eight more laws or rules for interpreting the Bible, and Christians often misunderstand the Bible because they do not use the

---

10. Claude Duval Cole, *Definitions of Doctrines* 1 (Mortons Gap, Kentucky: First Baptist Church, 1944), 101–102.

laws of interpretation.[11] To interpret the Old Testament by the New Testament is very important when we study the subject of the *mercy seat* because God designed the New Testament to explain the Old. Again, Dr. Cole comments:

> The New Testament mercy seat is not a place but a person, the Lord Jesus Christ. There is no place to which a sinner can flee to escape the justice of God. Men may flee to other countries to escape the judgment of human courts, but there are no fugitives from divine justice. God has jurisdiction in all countries, for he is judge of all the earth. There are no sacred spots of mercy on this earth. Salvation is not a matter of geography. If one could find the very tomb in which Jesus lay, and hide in it in the hope of mercy, the hounds of justice would find and punish him. A sinner might kneel at the very foot of the cross of wood on which Jesus died and yet not find mercy with God. The Lord Jesus Christ is the true mercy seat and sinners must flee to him for mercy.
>
> The very word that describes the Old Testament mercy seat (Hebrews 9:5) is applied to Christ in Romans 3:25: "Whom God hath set forth to be a propitiation (mercy seat) through faith in his blood." The word means that which appeases the wrath of God. Christ made appeasement by bearing the wrath of God on the Cross.
>
> The wrath due us fell on him. The mercy seat, therefore, is Christ in his atoning death. He could not remain in glory and be our mercy seat. He could not be a mercy seat in his infancy or as a man going about doing good. His vicarious death was an absolute necessity. He was speaking of himself when he said, "Except a corn of wheat fall into the ground and die, it abideth alone; but if it die, it bringeth forth much fruit" (John 12:24).

---

11. For more information on biblical interpretation, see George Bowman's book, *Ten Keys to Help You Interpret the Bible,* available from the author.

There is no physical approach to Christ, the true mercy seat. It is a mental and a heart approach. If the mercy seat were a material object like a seat of wood, stone, or gold, then the approach would be physical. We come to Christ, the true mercy seat, when we look to him and trust him for acceptance with God.[12]

THE DIVISIONS OF MERCY

God's Mercy Is General

Mercy arises from God's sovereign, imperial pleasure. Since mercy is one of God's wonderful, marvelous, unfathomable attributes, it varies and is different in regard to many of his subjects and creations. In other words, there are divisions of mercy. They are *general mercy, special mercy,* and *sovereign mercy.*

General mercy is not only extended to all men, believers and unbelievers alike, but to the entire creation. "His tender mercies," says the psalmist, "are over all his works" (Psalm 145:9). Paul the Apostle taught the same truth when he preached on Mars Hill in Athens, Greece. Addressing the Athenian philosophers who thought they were the leaders in human knowledge, he said that God "giveth to all life, and breath, and all things" (Acts 17:25). God also has pity upon the brute creation in their needs and supplies them with suitable provision.

God's Mercy Is Special

God exercises his special mercy towards the children of men, helping them and succouring them, their offensive sins notwithstanding. For them he provides the necessities of life. Jesus said that God "maketh the sun to rise on the evil and the good, and sendeth rain on the just and the unjust" (Matthew 5:45).

The mercies bestowed on the wicked, however, are of a temporal nature. They are confined strictly to this present life. Those who have an idea there will be a second chance, as it were, after they die are

---

12. Claude Duval Cole, *Definitions of Doctrines* 1 (Mortons Gap, Kentucky: First Baptist Church, 1944), 102–103.

in for shock of great disappointment. God will extend no mercy to them beyond the grave. "It is a people of no understanding," said the prophet: "Therefore he that formed them will show them no favour" (Isaiah 27:11).

God's Mercy Is Sovereign

God reserves his sovereign mercy, for the heirs of salvation which he communicates to them through the Mediator, the Lord Jesus Christ. Sovereign grace alone determines the exercise of divine mercy, for he saith to Moses, "I will have mercy on whom I will have mercy, and I will have compassion on whom I will have compassion. So then it is not of him that willeth, nor of him that runneth, but of God that sheweth mercy" (Romans 9:15–16).

The wretchedness of the creature does not cause God to show mercy because God is not influenced by things outside of himself. If God were influenced by the abject misery of sinners, he would cleanse and save them all. But he does not, and here's why: It is not his pleasure and purpose to do so. Our works, merits, and character cannot move God to save us because the Bible says, "Not by works of righteousness which we have done, but according to his mercy he saved us" (Titus 3:5).

Furthermore, the merits of Christ do not move God to bestow mercies on his elect. That would be putting the effect before the cause. Christ came "to give knowledge of salvation unto his people by the remission of their sins, through the tender mercy of our God; whereby the dayspring from on high hath visited us" (Luke 1:78–79). Mercy arises from God's sovereignty and good pleasure.

God's Mercy in Punishment

The Bible says that punishment can be an act of mercy. Failing to learn the laws for interpretation, some Christians have difficulty understanding these verses: "To him that smote Egypt in their firstborn: for his mercy endureth forever . . . but overthrew Pharaoh in the Red Sea: for his mercy endureth forever. . . . To him who smote great kings:

for his mercy endureth forever" (Psalm 136:10,15,17). Even casting the reprobates into the lake of fire is an act of mercy. How?

From God's side, his actions are an act of justice vindicating his honor. The mercy of God is never shown to the prejudice of his holiness and righteousness. In the exercise of his mercy he never violates his justice.

From the sinner's standpoint justice is an act of equity. He suffers the due reward of his iniquities. One preacher said, "Every sinner will go to hell satisfied that he is getting exactly what he deserves." From the vantage point of the redeemed, it is an act of mercy because it removes the evil order of things—blasphemy, crime, and offences of all kinds—as they are now. The Bible says of heaven, "And there shall in no wise enter into it anything that defileth, neither whatsoever worketh abomination, or maketh a lie; but they which are written in the Lamb's book of life" (Revelation 21:27).

The Bible also says, "And after these things I heard a great voice of much people in heaven, saying Alleluia; Salvation, and glory, and honor, and power, unto the Lord our God: For true and righteous are his judgments: for he hath judged the great whore, which did corrupt the earth with her fornication, and hath avenged the blood of his servants at her hand. And again they said, Alleluia And her smoke rose up forever and ever" (Revelation 19:1–3).

How foolish are the wicked unbelievers who hope that God is too merciful to send sinners to suffer in hell! "God is a loving and merciful God," they say. "He would never send his own human creatures to a place of suffering." But that is not what the Bible says. "The wicked," it says, "shall be turned into hell, and all the nations that forget God" (Psalm 9:17).

God's Mercy in My Family

God's mercy is widespread towards man, yet it is also very personal. It seems the Lord is especially concerned with showing mercy in the special institution he ordained for us, the family (see Psalm 68:6). Since this book is dedicated to my six children, to end this chapter and conclude this book here are a few family experiences that prove that God's mercy and goodness are the hounds of heaven.

Bob, our oldest son, had just turned sixteen years-old when he had an accident on a railroad track that *totaled* our station wagon. He and a neighbor's son escaped with bruises and cuts and did not have to be hospitalized. My second son David incurred a broken shoulder in the accident and had to remain in the hospital. The hounds of heaven, goodness and mercy, were close that afternoon. Bob later suffered a nervous breakdown in graduate school and was hospitalized for thirteen years. Today he is married, has a responsible job, a Christian wife, and three children.

David also had three other automobile accidents in which the cars were totaled and suffered broken ribs twice, as well as a punctured lung, and had to spend weeks on a hospital bed in our living room. After college and dental school, he rededicated his life to the Lord and became a dentist on a navy ship. Since then he has made nine dental trips to missionary posts in Central and South America.

When our oldest daughter, Barbara, was just a small girl, she climbed over the front seat of our car to get in the back seat. We were traveling at sixty miles per hour. In those days there were no car locks, safety precautions, or seatbelts engineered into automobiles.

Barbara stepped on the back door handle and the door flew open. By the providence of God, she was wearing a winter coat and my wife was riding in the back seat. As Barbara began to roll out through the open door, my wife made a lunge toward her, grabbed her winter coat, and screamed. Looking through the rear vision mirror, I could see what was happening so I slowed the car down as quickly as possible. We stopped, we cried, we prayed, and we thanked God. In that moment, we could truly hear the hounds of heaven barking!

When my wife was seven and a half months pregnant with our fourth child Bonnie, she slipped on the icy back porch of our parsonage in New York State, falling backwards down all the steps. She cracked her coccyx bone (as was discovered after the baby's birth) and was in terrible pain, having to sit on an air cushion for the last six weeks of her pregnancy. The doctor and the family were uncertain as to the condition of the unborn baby so there was much prayer during those six weeks. The baby was born with no ill effects at all from the fall. Again we thanked the Lord for the hounds of heaven—his goodness and mercy.

In case you think the hounds of heaven save only from death, the life of Douglas, our fifth child, unfolds like a fairy tale. He married his childhood sweetheart, Michele. They started going together in kindergarten! Michele has used her God-given intelligence for God's glory. She is one of the country's leading research pharmacists and she and Douglas own their own drug company.

Through their love, generosity, and philanthropy, they are educating thirteen nephews and nieces, giving scholarships to two colleges, as well as sending contributions to evangelistic efforts in America and the foreign mission field. The hounds of heaven have not only blessed them, but have followed trails to both sides of the family and scores of other persons among their close contacts.

When our youngest child was eight months old we left him with good church members while the rest of our family attended a summer camp at which I had been invited to speak. Upon our arrival home, we discovered that Danny had been taken to the hospital and was packed in ice. His temperature was between 106 and 107 degrees Fahrenheit!

At the hospital a Christian pediatrician, who had sat up all night with our son, said, "Pastor McNeill, I am afraid if he lives his brain will be damaged. I had only one other child with a temperature this high who lived."

I went home, went to the bedroom, got down on my knees, and prayed that God would take him in the next few hours if his brain was going to be severely damaged. Then something happened that has never occurred to me before or since. I didn't see a vision or hear a voice, but I was sure that the triune God had answered my prayer while I was on my knees.

Walking into the kitchen, where my wife, in tears, was trying to get supper ready, I said, "Quit crying, quit worrying. God has given me the assurance that if Danny lives his brain will not be affected one iota." In a few days the crisis was over. Danny lived and became well. Those hounds of heaven had once again visited the McNeill household!

God's Mercy in Suffering

Perhaps someone is saying, "You have been blessed beyond all measure, but what about those believers who have been tortured, suffered agony, and then martyred? Surely goodness and mercy did not follow them all their lives. What about the Christians who have had cancer and have lingered months, years, in a nursing home or hospital before dying? How could one say that the *hounds of heaven* are following them?"

I still believe that Psalm 23:6 is true of every believer who, in spite of suffering and tribulations, can say, "Surely goodness and mercy shall follow me all the days of my life: and I will dwell in the house of the LORD for ever." The moment a person receives Christ as his Lord and Saviour, this is positive proof that God's goodness and mercy have been following him since birth.

We often forget God's providence in his watchcare over his elect *before* their regeneration and conversion. God sometimes keeps his elect physically alive and mentally alert for years before the time he has chosen to call and regenerate them.

The thief on the Cross who was crucified beside Christ was a hardened sinner who was dying an excruciatingly painful death. He lived only a few hours after receiving Christ as his Lord and Saviour, but would anyone deny that the hounds of heaven were following him? Breathing his last, he could have rightly applied these words to himself: "Surely goodness and mercy shall follow me all the days of my life: and I will dwell in the house of the LORD for ever."

The twenty-third Psalm is one of the most beautiful passages in the Bible. To encourage you to take a renewed interest in and gain a renewed understanding of the Shepherd Psalm, here is what G. Campbell Morgan, that distinguished expositor of the Bible, had to say about it:

> This Psalm has one theme. I think it may be expressed thus: the sufficiency of God for all human need. It is indeed an unruffled song of rest. All the circumstances of our pilgrimage, want and weariness, wanderings and perplexities, the shadowed mysteries of the valleys, and the thronging enemies, and the infinite beyond are recognized as we make our way through the song. Want is cancelled, weariness finds a resting place in green pastures. Through perplexity there is guidance, and finally, the path runs on until it ends, not in a tangled wilderness, but in the King's palace.[13]

It would be difficult to improve on that description of the Shepherd Psalm. So we'll close by saying, Thank God for the twenty-third Psalm—especially the sixth verse, which contains our Lord's promise of the hounds of heaven—his goodness and mercy that shall follow us all the days of our lives. And may our gracious God use this book to encourage you to increase in holiness of life to the praise of his glorious grace.

---

13. G. Campbell Morgan, *Great Chapters of the Bible* (Grand Rapids: Flemming H. Revell), 55.

NOTES

NOTES

NOTES

NOTES

NOTES

NOTES

To order additional copies of

Unusual Topics

Have your credit card ready and call

Toll free: (877) 421-READ (7323)

or send $18.00* each plus $5.95 S&H**

to
**WinePress Publishing
PO Box 428
Enumclaw, WA 98022**

or order online at:
www.winepresspub.com

*Washington residents please add 8.5% tax.
**Add $1.50 S&H for each additional book ordered.